MYSELF | PASSING BY

a memoir in moments

Myself Passing By
First published November 2000
New Island Books
2 Brookside, Dundrum Road
Dublin 14

ISBN 1 902602 01 3

British Library Cataloguing in Publication Data
A catalogue record for this book is available
from the British Library

The Arts Council
An Chomhairle Ealaíon

New Island received financial assistance from The Arts Council
(An Chomhairle Ealaíon), Dublin, Ireland.

Cover design: Slick Fish Design, Dublin
Printed in Ireland by Colour Books, Dublin

MYSELF | PASSING BY

a memoir in moments

PETER JANKOWSKY

**NEW
ISLAND**

Born in Berlin in 1939, Peter Jankowsky worked for ten years as a professional actor there and in West Germany. Since 1971 he has lived in Dublin where he teaches German at the Goethe Institute. A regular contributor to RTÉ's *Sunday Miscellany*, he has also appeared in such RTÉ TV productions as *Caught in a Free State* and *Glenroe*. His translation, together with Brian Lynch, of Paul Celan's *65 Poems* was published in 1985, and another collaboration with Brian Lynch resulted in *Easter Snow/Osterschnee,* a book of photographs, poems and translations which was published in 1993. He has also translated a number of other Irish poets into German.

Contents

Part IV
Having Arrived

For you

Das Blatt im Wind
kennt seinen Weg

The leaf in the wind
knows its way

Foreword

In 1995 a new producer was appointed to RTÉ's *Sunday Miscellany*. She flung the doors wide open and introduced hundreds of new voices to the programme's large audience. One of them was mine. I was invited to submit a contribution, and since then there hasn't been a time when my mind was not occupied with one or several of these pieces. What began with a commission turned into an obsession. The present book therefore represents the backbone of my creative life since then.

Although I had already done a number of Interval Talks for RTÉ Radio — some of which are included in this book — it came as a shock to me to be asked to participate in a radio programme I had always regarded, and admired, as quintessentially Irish. It's difficult enough to produce something acceptable in your own language; to do so in a second language, of which you have only a limited command, is a never-ending and, at times, nerve-racking adventure. But who is not grateful for an adventure? Also, as I write this, I realise that I cannot imagine how I could have composed these pieces in my mother tongue; the idea is almost unthinkable. Poems, on the other hand, would only ever come to me in German. Over the years of writing these radio pieces, I have found that their genesis was not unlike the way poems come into being — the transformation of experience into word-work happens at all kinds of speed, spontaneously or after life-long gestation: 'Ramona' was scribbled down straight after the event, while 'The Enamel Jug' had to wait half a century. So, despite being rooted in the same fund of experience, the poems and the radio pieces arose, unfailingly, in different languages, as if each of these had its unique access to that selfsame store. Perhaps one is even a different person in another language. Sometimes, as I wrote these stories, a freshness and a freedom stirred in me which I think must be distantly related to the intoxicating sense of liberation I experienced on my first journey to Ireland, in 1957, as an 18-year-old schoolboy.

When you're in your fifties, your past begins to burn. In my case that fire coincided with my participation in the radio programmes mentioned. Here I was given opportunities to make sense or, indeed, a nonsense of the memories that lay dormant in me, waiting for ignition. When so many others were forgotten, irretrievably lost, these moments had stayed with me, alive, colourful, recallable in many details. 'Leap-moments' I came to call them as they revisited me; opalescent instances, vibrant with hidden meaning, that leap out of or, maybe, into (from where?) the monochrome of an ordinary life.

Putting them together now in chronological order — the only sensible arrangement I could come up with — seems to suggest the outline of an autobiography.

That was unavoidable, I suppose, but never intended. Our lives are hardly the sum of radiant moments. Or are they?

Peter Jankowsky
Stillorgan, September 2000

Part I

Setting Out

From Hell to Paradise and Back

The summer of 1943 saw Berliners on the receiving end of the 'Total War' a selected number of them had clamoured for so frantically earlier that year. The bombing raids left tens of thousands of them homeless, wounded, killed. Panic set in; Goebbels issued an urgent appeal to everyone who was not bound to Berlin by work, to evacuate the city, especially women and children. That included my mother, already war widowed but now married again, my baby brother and myself, then four years old. In August 1943 we left for Peilau, a small village in Silesia, where distant relatives had offered us one room in their house. We exchanged the frightening city, where the nightly wailing of the air-raid sirens announced terror and death, for the Elysian fields of this distant countryside, where all the sights, sounds and smells were peaceful, and utterly new to the city child. It is there that my earliest memories come from; while I can recall only a single, blurred event from the time before our evacuation, there is, at the very bottom of my remembered life, a whole trove of vividly coloured episodes from these one-and-a-half years in the country. A change of environment seems to switch on the retaining capabilities of our brains.

It is still a mystery to me, however, why, of the innumerable exciting moments that make up a child's day and year, only a particular few stay in the mind. Is it due, perhaps, to extra emotional involvement? If so, why, when other equally joyful or tearful events are irretrievably lost? If there is a meaning in their undiminished presence in our minds — how can it be grasped? Are these earliest memories perhaps departure points of lines that run through our entire lives, collecting and connecting events of later years, and giving them the structure of necessity, of consequence? Like the anchoring points of a spider's web? Did my budding personality decide to retain these incidents, or did they themselves elect to stay alive and pulsing in my brain? Did they make me, or did I create them? How strong is the element of chance in all this? Questions, only giving rise to ever more questions.

Without having answers to these, I grope my way back to those 18 months in the countryside, when I woke up to the world in the long village of Peilau. 'Long' because it consisted of a large number of smallholdings strung along the road like pearls, *Straßendörfer*, road-villages, as they are called in Germany. Often several kilometres long, they have no real centre, although somewhere along the line will be a church, a school and a pub.

The people we stayed with were no farmers, though. Uncle Paul worked with a newspaper in the nearest town and was rarely ever on the scene. Aunt Mary and her little daughter Eva were the people we had to learn to get on with, which took some time — as refugees always have to overcome deep-seated reservations. For us children there was a garden with chickens and ducks, the rural landscape all around us and a completely new freedom for the young discoverer from the city.

From our fourth-floor apartment in Berlin I had come down to earth, in a literal sense. It must have been soon after our arrival that the potato and fodder-beet harvests took place. Now, this was paradise — not the miserable little sand-pits of our city playgrounds! — here you could plod around in an entire field, slowly building up thick soil soles under your shoes that weighed you down and lifted you simultaneously. And you just had to bite into the glistening surfaces of potatoes cut by the spade! The taste was disappointing, but for a moment you felt as if you were munching crystals. And the fodder-beet, weren't they just magnificent! Huge swelling pink bodies came out of the ground if you grasped their bundle of leaves with both hands and threw your whole weight into the pull. They resisted for a while, then slowly yielded, finally slipping out of the ground so suddenly that you were thrown back on your behind. All the other people who had been watching the city kid grappling burst into laughter and applause. That felt great! You were watched, the centre of attention, if you didn't mind the ridicule. So you put on the show again and again, and from knowing yourself in later years, were probably overdoing it a bit. The results were diminishing, but the act itself was its own reward, the intimate encounter with the heavy, moist soil and its wondrous fruit.

That soil is called *loess*, a rich, fertile loam, characteristic of such areas on the Eurasian continent. It was one of the reasons why Frederick II of Prussia, in three wars in the 18th century, with the loss of tens of thousands of soldiers, had annexed Silesia, adding it to his meagre, sandy heartland around Berlin, for which he was given the accolade of Frederick the Great. The same area, one hundred years later, saw great misery and famine as the Prussian authorities brutally suppressed a desperate revolt by starving weavers, the theme of Gerhart Hauptmann's *The Weavers*, Germany's first naturalistic drama. A dark historical back-drop to the bright innocence of my harvesting joys.

The *loess* plain was criss-crossed by country lanes which, after centuries of use by ox-cart, were cut deeply into the soft terrain, *Hohlwege*, hollow roads. They are often mentioned in Central-European poetry, as things of the heart tend to happen there, inescapable encounters, for better or for worse, slight occurrences that linger in the mind. To get to the house where we stayed, you had to pass along one of these sunken roads. It was a stimulating place and I often played there with Eva, the daughter of our hosts, a girl two or three years older than myself. Also in the neighbourhood lived an extremely poor family, gypsy-like people with a large number of children who seemed to be forever hungry and foraging for food. We had seen them picking up edible stuff from the road and, without examining it, put it into their mouths. This gave us an idea for a prank — we knew it was mean but we couldn't resist it. We took a ripe cherry, carefully removed the stone and replaced it with clay. Then, leaving it on the road where we knew the children would soon pass, we hid ourselves high on the shoulder of the sunken road. Everything worked according to our plan: they came, they saw the cherry, their eyes lit up, one of them stooped — and straight into his mouth went the doctored fruit. The next moment the happy face turned into a grimace, as he spat the lot out.

And we laughed. Yes, for an instant there was a weak upwelling of triumph, smothered immediately by an overwhelming, and still growing, sense of shame. Adam and Eva had sinned, truly sinned — they had misused the fruit of paradise for the pleasure of power over the poor and unsuspecting. I felt evil, for the first time, a most distinct and irrefutable feeling which, together with a few similarly repulsive acts in later life, has protected me from occasional attacks of moral superiority.

A demon of a different kind awoke in the five-year-old boy in that same, sun-kissed summer, as the adults gradually noted how he disappeared regularly in the direction of a certain farm, carrying childish gifts, a toy, for instance, or a single sweet. The reason why he persevered, despite the adults' gentle mocking, was the farmer's daughter, a girl probably three times his age, in her teens, anyway. He adored her, if that is the proper word for the sweetly searing wish to be in her presence that had somehow drenched his whole being. The time to be with Anneliese was when she attended the cows, in the warm, sweet-smelling twilight of the stable, fascinated by the girl's calm, deliberate dealings with the big animals, and entranced by the spell of female otherness. She was so assured, so strong, where he was so ignorant, so anxious, so much in need — of what, he only found out, by and by, in later years. Amused and maybe even a bit charmed by her youthful suitor, Anneliese didn't mind having him around; she gave him friendly words and thereby, without knowing it, his first experience of being where he belonged, where he was even more complete than in the presence of his mother. How long this tender attachment lasted I have forgotten, but that's where another of the paths that meander through my life began, in the unconsummated intimacy of that stable.

Nature broke out from within and broke in from without. One brilliant day in May we were brought into a grove of oak trees, not far from the house. After some moments we felt that something was wrong, the light, and the sounds, too. Where there should have been leaf-green shadows was a bare brightness, and the air was alive with an unsettling sizzling sound. The adults soon showed us: how trees had been denuded by thousands of May-bugs, or cockchafers, those pretty, inch-long, black, brown and white beetles German children used to keep as pets for a few weeks in early summer, when they could be shaken from trees or even bought in pet-shops. They sometimes appeared, in seven-year cycles, in huge, devastating numbers, we were told. And now we saw — the trees were encrusted with them, the forest floor carpeted with their crawling masses; you could not tread without crushing them. And that sizzling sound emanated from the movements of millions of jaws, limbs and papery wings. This was a biblical plague; the grown-ups mumbled and shouted as the peaceful, pastoral landscape of May suddenly changed its face — out of the middle of Eden there had risen this uncontrollable monster, threatening to overroll and swallow everything. It didn't, in the end; the danger ran its course and then subsided. But the child had received a glimpse of the other, the alien, the destructive side of nature. And there were even more frightening, more sinister insights into the nature of things and man to come for the child in those 18 months in the countryside.

The two winters we spent there were of the Continental kind, with lots of snow and hard frost. What did we children know about the millions who perished in those winters, at the front, in the bombed cities, in the concentration camps? We got our sledges out and made use of every slope, every little incline we could find in this level landscape. Once a group of local children, myself happily included, spent an afternoon tobogganing down the slope of that cockchafer grove, climbing up again, gliding down again — the whole breath-steaming afternoon long. Whether I had missed the call for the return home or had wanted just one more go — I suddenly found myself at the bottom of the hill, with my little sledge on a string and completely alone. Also, all at once, very tired. In order to get home I had to climb that slope, now icy and slippery from our sledges. The trees on the top loomed, bare and black, against a dark purple sky. I tried to ascend the slope, but after a few steps on the icy surface I slipped and slithered back to the bottom. I tried again, and slipped even sooner. I became afraid, and called out for the others. No one answered or came. Tears were welling up — tears had always been effective in procuring help. Not this time, though. In the frosty darkness closing in, I saw that I was alone, all alone, and had to take my rescue in my own hands — at least that's how I perceived the situation. And that required some thinking, the garnering of all my remaining strength, and a holding-on to all the will-power I hadn't known was in me. Slowly, sideways, step by step, hauling the sledge after me in long, desperate pulls, I made it to the top of the hill. The rewards were manifold, not least an instinctive understanding of how Sisyphus feels when he starts, once again, to roll his stone up the mountainside, and also a deep conviction of the enabling nature of loneliness.

Soon afterwards the winter turned so cold that we were only allowed to go outdoors for short spells and any movement in our village all but ceased. But one day we looked up at the long road — our house was situated slightly below it — we looked up and saw a terribly disquieting, inexplicable sight: an endless procession of beings staggering from right to left, south to north, on the snow-plastered, iced-over surface. They must have been human beings, because they wore striped pyjamas and had rags wrapped around their feet, but otherwise they were not recognisably human, so skeletal were their bodies, so hollow their faces, so hopeless the expression in their eyes as they slowly, slowly stumbled along.

And why were the other people, those well-fed, armed, uniformed men shouting at them, beating them with whips, trying to make them move faster, if only for a very few steps? What horror did we see before our eyes? The poor people, everyone said. But who were they? Surely they must be bad people who had done awful things, if they were punished like that. But there were so many of them, and the next day there were many, many more. Mum took me by the hand and brought me into the house, saying this was no sight for little children.

Later that evening we heard a villager whisper how one of those miserable people had managed to leave the procession unseen and had entered a house by the roadside. Finding the inhabitants peeling boiled potatoes, he had, 'like an animal!', the villager said, thrown himself over the bucket of peels, stuffing handfuls of them into his mouth. Then, leaving the house again, with a slice of bread the housewife had quickly slipped into his pocket, he had been spotted by one of the uniformed guards who, without uttering a word, put a pistol to his head and shot him dead. The ragged creature lay bleeding in the snow. Turning to the horrified farmer, the uniformed man had asked: 'Do you have a forkful of manure to cover that there?' And the farmer had answered no, but he did have some straw! Everyone among the listeners was full of admiration for this courageous reply. Today I know that what we had witnessed were the infamous Death Marches, when the surviving inmates of Auschwitz were herded, away from the approaching Soviet troops, towards the German heartland. It was January 1945, the end was in sight — where did the SS think they could take and hide them? Where could they hide themselves? That procession, seen when I was five years old, has continued making its way all through my life, if anything, the image clearer with the years.

Soon we too were travelling the frozen roads, without understanding, following orders, on foot, by horse-cart and tractor and a succession of trains. With some bundles and a suitcase, one child on her arm, another by the hand, my mother made her way back to Berlin — where else would she go? Berlin was home, war was by now everywhere. My memories of those days are hazy and confused, nights and days indistinguishable; yet one moment stands out: a woman had handed her baby into a train through a window, intending to force her way through one of the doors. But the train moved off, with the baby inside, as she was left behind, howling 'like an animal' — again I heard the adults use that expression. My mother put her own hands over my ears, but that howl will forever echo in there.

We arrived in Berlin late one evening, in the middle of an air-raid warning, and were immediately led into a huge underground shelter where hundreds already lay in huddled masses. We found ourselves an empty spot and promptly dropped into a bottomless sleep. When we awoke next morning, we found the room vacated. Somebody told us to leave the station and go to the hotel across the road where some food could be collected. We crossed the street. It was totally on fire. Black smoke rose from houses on both sides and merged above the burning roofs. Firefighters moved into this tunnel of smoke and flames, yelling, dragging water-hoses along. Tiles were crackling, burning timbers falling. We were back home, back in hell.

The Bomb Meant for Me

The air-raid sirens howl out. I know by now what I have to do: I grab Dutzeldatzel, my tiny teddy-bear, and, holding him tightly in my fist, I run ahead, down the four floors from our apartment in this block of flats in the centre of Berlin. Downstairs the backdoor of the hallway opens into a small, square courtyard, formed by the four wings of the building, and it's from there that a short flight of stairs leads to the air-raid shelter in the basement where the tenants are supposed to be protected from the bombs. Thousands, of course, have not survived the collapse of the houses above their heads, but I'm not aware of that as I leap down the stairs, scared without exactly knowing why. My mother follows as fast as she can, my little brother on one arm, a bundle of belongings under the other.

When I reach the open back door my eyes are drawn upwards by a mighty roar coming from the sky. For a moment, all I can see is a beautiful blue square of cloudless sky that stops me in my tracks — it's springtime now, April 1945, and the weather is glorious. Then a huge, silvery-dark bird flies diagonally across the blue square on outstretched wings — the first plane I've ever seen. As I gaze up in rapture, something dark drops from it, like a black egg, and falls straight towards my upturned face — a present meant especially for me. The next moment it has arrived, my whole world is shaken to its foundations, and I am gone.

The bomb had fallen into the dead centre of the courtyard, half-a-dozen steps away from me, in the flowerbed there. The soft soil had muffled the explosion, and the house still stood. Yet the pressure-wave had blown me back into the hallway, up a few steps, past my mother — 'Like a leaf whirling in the wind,' she described my passage later — and had let me down gently, if that is the word, at the other end of the hallway, on some sort of air-cushion that must have formed against the closed front door. I had passed out momentarily but was otherwise unharmed. Had I been standing just one step further out, the cataract of broken window-panes crashing down from four floors after the explosion would have cut me into pieces. Not to mention other ifs and eventualities …

There is an invisible line drawn, maybe in the air, maybe in the mind, maybe in the Nowhere, and if you step over it, unwittingly, the black egg hits you, and you are dead; but if you happen not to, there are motherly kisses, and tears of relief; and a few days afterwards the war is over, and the first day of peace coincides with my birthday. I'm six years old now and soon will have to go to school, and a whole life stretches before me.

The End of a War

There it was, the dreaded hard knock on the door. My grandmother opened it and, yes, there was a Russian soldier outside, just one, a fairly young one too, maybe in his early twenties. Fully armed. He uttered just one word: *Matka*! We knew that was what they said when they demanded women to come forward. For the last few days now, after the conquest of Berlin and the end of the war, there were terrible rumours around, many of them certainly true, others the after-effects of years of Third Reich propaganda. When we were still in the air-raid shelters and Russian officers had come to check on us, the younger women always hid themselves as best as they could and took great pains to appear as old and ugly as possible. Women know instinctively from a million years of experience what to expect from the victors in a conflict. Still — the first those 'sub-human hordes from the steppes of inner Asia' had done in our district was to establish field-kitchens to feed the children of yesterday's enemy.

And now this single soldier had climbed all the way up to our top-floor apartment in search of a woman. My granny was over 60 years old, white-haired and nicely shrivelled, surely she was out of the question. She said firmly: Nix Matka here! And was about to slam the door shut. But at that moment my little two-year-old brother and myself, in our innocence and curiosity, peeped around the corner and he saw us. Granny could not possibly be the mother of these young children. In a flash the soldier had put his foot in the door, pushed it open and snatched up my little brother. Without a word he turned around and walked down the stairs to the landing where a tall window overlooked the courtyard, three-and-a-half floors below. An exploding bomb had shattered all the glass in the house a few days before, and now the monster stood there, close to the low sill of the gaping window, looking down ominously, the child on his right arm.

By now my mother had come out of her hiding, as she, Granny and I stared at the soldier. It was the month of May, and the sun was streaming down on the pair at the window, the man in uniform with his smooth, youthful face and my baby brother with his glistening blond curls. What was going on? From the context we could only assume that he was blackmailing my mother, even I could sense that. Was he threatening to drop the child unless …? The two women were whispering and whimpering, their urge to go to the child countered by their fear of endangering him further. None of us had a word of Russian. The soldier stood and stared, my brother all the time remained quite calm. When the soldier moved his left arm, we held our breath — but he only put his hand on the boy's hands and let it rest there, as if to protect him with his left arm from the intentions of the right. He stood there for a little while longer, very still, gazing down into the void, his face inclined slightly towards the child's hair. Then, with sudden resolution, he stirred, bent down, set my brother on the floor and, without looking back, walked down the stairs. And was gone. My mother rushed down, picked up her child and held him in her arms. Not unlike the soldier, a moment ago.

The Enamel Jug

In winter the playground of the kindergarten was reduced to a few grassy square metres that rose just above the low-lying ground, the remnant of a number of allotments that from autumn onwards turned into a muddy morass. All around this mud-field loomed the typical four-storey houses of Berlin, many of them now ruins. That was the horizon the children saw every day. A group of them were playing on the little patch of green: five- and six-year-olds, half-a-dozen girls and a single boy. It wasn't peaceful play, it consisted of chases and scuffles, the girls nagging the boy, he making them scream by pulling their sleeves and their hair — all bitterly enjoyable in the dim November light of the first winter after the end of the war.

Unnoticed by the playing children another boy appeared on the scene, like an emanation out of their grim surroundings, a tall, scraggy lad of, maybe, 14 years, poorly dressed in something uniform-like that hung greenish-grey down from his bony shoulders, as did his long arms. His right hand clutched the handle of an enamel jug, the kind you would take to a field-kitchen for a ladleful of soup. He stood there motionless, watching, his pale face without expression.

The little boy had just burst into a wild dervish dance, flailing his arms and making the girls scatter and screech, when the din was cut, as if by a blade, by the strange boy's voice: 'Look away!' he ordered the girls firmly. The children all stopped their play and looked at him. The small boy stood in front of the tall one, his eyes on him in wonderment. He saw him raise his right arm slowly, the handle of the chipped enamel jug clenched in his fist, he saw him swing his arm back as far as he could. And then the tall boy, with all his might, brought the pot down on the little boy's head, striking just above his right eyebrow and cutting down to the bone. They all could hear the short, hard knock, as if on wood, the little boy heard it from within. Blood spurted; then, after a moment of silent shock, came a howl, more of horror than pain. Fingers covering the violated face were flooded with blood, saliva and tears. He stumbled forward, calling for the kindergarten nurse, the girls fluttering all around him, screaming now with genuine terror. They completely forgot about the other boy who had vanished, unseen, back to from where he had first appeared, the war-torn city. The bleeding boy was brought to a first-aid station in the neighbourhood. The wound needed a few stitches, and with a big bandage around his head, like a turban, he was then delivered home into the arms of mother and grandmother.

And that's where that day ended for me — in a nest of warmth and nourishment and care. Where did the tall boy go? Where had he come from? For half a century now his darkly looming figure, his right arm swung back, has been a regular visitor to my sleepless hours. Why had he wanted to erase me from his world? For that had been his intention, I have no doubt about that; had he had an axe instead of that enamel jug, he would have used it, such was his wilful ferocity. Over the years I have brooded over the few details I still remember. Those uniform bits, for instance. Had he perhaps been one of the unfortunate teenage boys the Nazis had drafted at the very end of the war, teaching them to kill, to be heroic, to defend their mothers and sisters? Had he, in his confused mind, wanted to rescue those little girls from their tormentor? Even then I had dimly felt that jealousy had been a motive, not so much of my being with girls, but of my not being alone. And that pitiful enamel jug — had he no one to feed him, were his parents dead, maybe still buried under the rubble? Was he merely roaming around, homeless, gone feral, after all he had seen, all he had lost? Was he, when we met, as impregnated with death as I was as yet unmarked by it? I will never have answers to these questions, but over a lifetime, I feel, they have brought me ever closer to him, my would-be executioner, my older brother, Cain.

Creating Hippos and Giraffes

The city I had come from was in a sorry state in 1947: ruins and rubble everywhere, including the houses that remained standing; families in tatters, ruined bodies, minds in pieces. Two very cold winters had threatened with hunger and frost, the following, unusually hot summers with epidemics, polio a particular problem. If possible, children were sent to the countryside, and that was why I now found myself in a small village in Thuringia, in the heart of Germany. I couldn't believe my eyes when I arrived: not a single ruin in sight! The houses huddled together around the church and churchyard, themselves surrounded by a patchwork of many-sized, multi-coloured fields. Roads lined with apple trees led to other villages beyond the hilly horizon. A timeless picture-book village then, in 1947, at least for a child, a place where life had gone on undesecrated, uninterrupted, it seemed — the very counter-world to the one I had come from.

There were also animals everywhere, to my inexhaustible joy. I lost my heart to the goat kids, I was in awe of the big, warm bulk of the cows, their spiky horns. And I soon had to develop a special relationship with geese, for after a few days of finding my feet in my new environment, I was made a goose-herd and had to bring a flock of 20 or 30 geese out to the harvested fields for them to feed on the gleanings. My days were busy from morning till nightfall; I think I was as happy and fulfilled then as any child can be in this world.

Great was my surprise therefore when I discovered that even in this world so brimful with reality something was lacking — and that I was the one who could supply what was missing. It wasn't much, really, but just as my world had been opened up by my coming to Thuringia, so I now held the key to open the door to the outside world for someone in the village.

Alfons was an only child in the family where I stayed, a boy of seven, exactly one year younger than myself. He and I slept in the same bed at night and before we fell asleep we talked in the pitch-black darkness of our bedroom. My favourite subject was animals. Alfons knew everything about the animals of his world — they were nothing to him — but it turned out that he barely knew the names, not to mention the appearance, of more exotic animals, such as those I had seen in the badly bombed-out, but still functioning, Berlin Zoo. And he couldn't get enough of my description of these animals.

In some cases this was very easy. A zebra? A horse with black-and-white stripes all over! Alfons giggled. Gazelles and antelopes? Ah well, beige-coloured goats and sheep, more or less. A crocodile? A huge lizard, as big, oh, even bigger than our bed! Alfons shuddered and never again asked about the crocodile. But for my word-paintings of the other animals he asked again and again. I suppose it was the first time his imagination was fed, and challenged. And challenged, too, were my powers of description. Instinctively I followed the basic rule of all teaching: Begin with the known, proceed to the unknown!

What does a giraffe look like? Well, Alfons, think of a cow! Have you got the cow? — Yes! — Now pull the head of the cow up, so that the neck gets longer and longer, really long! OK, that should be long enough. Now take each leg and pull, so that it becomes a really long leg, each one of them, right? — Yes! — Now, what you've got there is a giraffe! Alfons worked hard imagining, and what he saw, made him speechless.

The next task was a hippopotamus or Nile-horse, as it's called in German. But a horse was no help here, so the poor cow had to come in again to assist me, this time to be blown up, shortened, compressed, equipped with a blubbery skin, protruding eyes and horrible tusks. Alfons was shaken but asked me to go on. And so I leave it to the reader's imaginative powers to envision all the mental manipulations it takes to transform the humble pig into an elephant.

Night after night we remade a small part of creation out of nothing but words. Sometimes I wonder what Alfons may have actually visualised in the dark, what monsters followed him into his dreams. What becomes of our words once they are spoken? That's always the question between narrator and listener or reader, isn't it? Even at this very moment.

Cold War and Warmth

For a year or so the air over Berlin was thick with planes —
on average there was one landing every 90 seconds. Wall-
shattering noise, especially for those of us living near the
airport, but welcome, reassuring, life-giving noise all the
same. The time was 1948-9, and Berlin was under blockade.
The Cold War was well and truly under way. Food, fuel and
medical supplies could only be provided by scores of
American and British pilots who flew bravely and tirelessly
across the Soviet-occupied Eastern Zone of Germany, thereby
connecting the three blocked-off Western Sectors of Berlin
with the Western world at large.

The four members of my family, huddled together in the
kitchen of our small flat on the fourth floor, certainly didn't
mind the roar above the roof. Busy with everyday toil, even
the two adults were largely unaware of the historical
significance of their plight. Unaware — but not blissfully so:
the flat was dark, there were only two to four hours of
electricity per day, and it was cold, as every household
received only 30 pounds of coal for that entire winter. My
grandmother and my mother needed all their ingenuity and
self-sacrifice to keep things going for two boys of nine and
five years respectively. Imagination was a vital resource in
those times, never more so, and more literally so, than in the
long, cold winter nights, when we nestled close to each other

in the dwindling warmth of the kitchen stove or, later, in bed, where the two warm female bodies cradled us like a nest. What do human beings do in the cold and darkness of their caves? They talk, they recite, they rhyme and riddle, and they sing. My grandmother seemed to us to have an inexhaustible treasure — and that was the word! — a treasure of stories, ballads, jokes and puzzles, and she was a natural story-teller and lover of words to boot. Thus poetry for me was, from the outset, intimately connected with togetherness and sharing, with shelter and endurance, even survival, offering bright images against a cold, dark world.

My mother too had her moments of stardom — in a charmingly real sense — a song she had in which people talk to a star in the night sky and the star replies to them. It was the most beautiful singing I knew when my mother answered our question of how she was? 'Quite well — safe in the care of God's hands!' she sang, but then I could only compare her sweet, girlish soprano with the barking baritone of the lady in the kindergarten. Even more entrancing was a Christmas poem she knew which began with the lines: 'The stars shine brightly far, far across the land' and which contained some magically repetitive verses:

> *Und die sich hart bekriegen, sollen einander verzeihn,*
> *Und die in Ketten liegen, sollen gerettet sein.*
> *Und die in Nacht verzagen, soll Himmelslicht erbaun,*
> *Und die da Heimweh tragen, sollen die Heimat schaun.*

Which is:

> And those waging war shall forgive each other,
> And those lying in chains shall be released.

And those in dark despair shall see a heavenly light,
And those yearning for home, they shall be given a home!

Little did I understand then how these lines promised relief from the great scourges of human existence — war, enslavement, spiritual despair and homelessness — nor that those words had a very real bearing on our own situation. But poetry was not a matter of understanding then, it was food for minds as hungry as the body. You don't *understand* bread when you eat it. Or maybe you do. And so I asked for the poem again and again in those long, dark winter nights, learning it, and all the others, by *heart*, as it were, while world history was passing overhead, unnoticed and unnoticing, on cold metal wings.

Good Hands

Not all the bombs dropped on my hometown did explode, many just plopped into the ground and waited there to be unearthed by pickaxe or shovel — and for a second chance to wreak devastation. When after the war workers came across yet another one of these blind bombs, everyone dropped their tools; the area was cordoned off, people were evacuated and the *Polizeifeuerwerker* called in, the bomb disposal unit of the Berlin police. In my time it consisted of just two men, Räbiger and Stefan — who were always mentioned together, like Castor and Pollux or Laurel and Hardy. An eerie silence descended on the area while they were at their job, people stopped whatever they were doing and just stared and listened, the seconds ticking away heavily, until the sirens sounded the 'all clear'; the two had done it again and everything returned to normal. Often we saw photographs of them in our newspaper, looking up at the camera from the bottom of a deep hole in the rubble, dwarfed by one of those huge, rusty, rotten eggs they had rendered harmless.

What kind of people were these men? What was it like to spend one's working life just the trembling of a hand away from total oblivion? I was then one of the amateur journalists editing our school magazine *Die Lupe* (*The Magnifying-Glass*), and so I commissioned myself to find the answers to these questions. My application to Police Headquarters received a reluctant but positive reply: Normally not — but they would make an exception for a school magazine. And please — no sensationalising! They needn't have worried.

Two weeks later I was sitting across from Mr Räbiger, the senior of the two-man squad. His superior was also present, to keep an eye on things, in a gesture, I felt, of both pride and protection. Räbiger was not in his usual overalls as I had naively expected but in what looked like his Sunday uniform. He was obviously uncomfortable and embarrassed by the situation, as was I, of course, facing one of the city's most popular heroes. To be honest, he didn't cut a very dashing figure: a small, middle-aged, compact man with a neatly parted cap of dark hair and small, dark, quiet eyes. An animal came to mind — yes, the sloth I had seen in the zoo, moving slowly, imperceptibly, upside-down, along a branch. Or some other secretive mammal, its gleaming black eyes watching you from within a shadowy hole.

The interview turned out to be heavy-going. Räbiger was not a man of words, given to psychological analysis. My rather gauche teenage questions produced awkward replies — No, they couldn't afford to be nervous ... they prepared themselves as well as they could ... it was a job that had to be done — that sort of thing. Soon I ran out of questions. The silence emanating from Mr Räbiger was about to engulf the stuffy little room, when the superior came to the rescue — Why not show the young man some of the tools they used? Räbiger calmly agreed and opened his toolbox, taking out one instrument after another and giving its name and purpose. And then silently looked at the thing for a few seconds before putting it back, carefully, in its proper place. They were all coated in lead, he said, to prevent sparks. Lead, I thought, was the word: a dull colour, great weight and no sparks at all.

And then my interview was over. A farewell handshake, and I was back on the street. Rather crestfallen, I had to admit. How to write an exciting piece for the *Lupe* on the basis of such a dud of an interview? But then a memory rose in me, took hold of my consciousness, and has remained there ever since: that final handshake! Not a shake at all, in fact the total opposite — as if my hand had been gripped by one of the vices he had shown me, the pressure increasing gradually, up to a painful pitch, and then again, ever so slowly and evenly, waning until my hand had been released. And there had been absolutely nothing demonstrative about it, I realised; rather his hand had told me everything I had wanted to know, his mind, his craft, his secret. It had even given me, as a representative of his community, a reassurance for the future: here was a man of poor words, but with good hands.

My Eroica

When a friend recently presented me with a book on the many islands off the British mainland island, my first reaction was automatic: I looked for the entry on Skomer, the only one among them that has a personal meaning for me. It is a rocky island off the Welsh coast, at the mouth of the Bristol Channel, a nature reserve which, some years ago, was in the news after it had suffered damage to its wildlife following an oil disaster in the Channel. Skomer is visited nowadays by large numbers of day-trippers and, right enough, there was a photograph in the book of a group of them, in red and yellow rain-gear, looking down from a cliff-top into a narrow inlet called Seal Cove. My heart beat faster as I read the text on Skomer, which included warnings about the crumbling edges of the cliffs, due to the nibbling of thousands of rabbits that had reduced 'the top covering of the island to a funnelled tissue of fragility'. It was painful reading for me. Was it possible that there were clues here to a more than 40-year-old mystery? A wave of emotion washed over me, its origin a few days in the distant past, a time suffused with a shimmering light, but ending in a sudden eclipse. And both the light and darkening emanated from a name which, given a different set of events, could have had considerable impact in Ireland, but which today probably nobody here remembers — that of Karl-Ernst Schünemann.

So, for another start to my story, I have to go back to my secondary school days in Berlin. To make up for the paucity of cultural stimuli in our deprived area, our school regularly invited in various acts and personalities — I remember Gluck's *Orpheus and Eurydice*, performed by a small ensemble of travelling opera-singers, a desperately hilarious experience for us young ignoramuses who couldn't get over the flashing of a gold front-tooth in the mouth of the fat lady who sang the role of Orpheus. On another occasion Willy Brandt, at that time Lord Mayor of West Berlin, came for a question-and-answer session on the workings of parliamentary democracy, while another endless morning was spent listening to an aged zoologist talking incessantly about his discoveries in the adventure-book world of the unimaginably distant Dark Continent. But there was also the tall, blond young man who came to us three times, and whose visits were eagerly awaited by everyone. Karl-Ernst Schünemann was our hero, in his company we came to know the wildernesses of northern Scandinavia — a faraway region for us, before the days of Interrail tickets and mass tourism. For Karl-Ernst had, all on his own, walked the boggy, mosquito-infested expanses of the tundra, had lived with the nomadic Lapps, the reindeer people, and camped for weeks on end on a narrow ledge in the cliff-face of a bird-rock in the Viking world of the Lofoten Islands, determined to photograph the elusive white-tailed eagle. For us boys he was the incarnation of all our dreams of lonely, daring self-discovery in an world of imminent danger and daily challenge. The girls, too, admired him for all the right reasons, but there was no denying he was also very good-looking, with a smile that lit up our drab assembly hall, along with a gentle voice and manner, a sense of humour, and a

genuine enthusiasm in sharing his experiences with us,
although he certainly had spoken in dozens of other schools
before. He also had a bright, natural intelligence, but he was
no intellectual; there was no speculative barrier between him
and us, making the effect his presence had on us all the more
like music in its immediacy. And the tune we heard was very
alluring.

Central to his success, of course, were the colour-slides
which formed the backbone of his talks. It's probably
impossible to convey to young people of today the
overwhelming effect slide-shows had in those days. The visual
exploitation of the world was only just beginning, colour TV
was unknown, colour photography rare, our surroundings
were not as yet awash with sensational images. A slide-show
was a revelation, a window into undreamt-of worlds. I can still
hear the Ohs! and Ahs! which greeted many of those radiant
images when they burst onto the screen.

Karl-Ernst was one of us, a fellow Berliner — yet he had
conquered that distant, colourful world, and in so doing
opened doors to our imagination, doors of possibilities, which
many of us went through, if only to escape for a couple of
weeks those black-and-white years in post-war Berlin. What's
more, the gradual increase in motor traffic presented us with a
novel way of long-distance journeying — hitchhiking —
making us the first generation of young Germans who
'tramped', as we called it, in growing numbers to the far ends
of Europe; many of us Berliners followed Karl-Ernst's
footsteps to the extreme north of the Continent. And that was
the main reason why, in the summer of 1957, I spent my
holidays in Ireland: I wanted to discover my own country, and
I wanted to be able to talk to its people. Some poems by W.B.

Yeats and some intriguing photographs of ancient stone structures also played their part in my decision, and there was surely something fateful and irrational to it as well.

So now I have to begin my story for a third time: after a week or so of hitchhiking, I arrived in Dun Laoghaire, and then headed straight for antiquity. Tara Hill, in pouring rain, was less than impressive, but Newgrange, then only an inconspicuous hillock in a green landscape, made up for it; I had to track down a farmer who kept the key to the monument and was then left alone, in mid season, with my torch, deep in the bowels of the mound. Next was Mellifont Abbey, in the throes of excavation and preservation by the monks. A day later, on my way to Monasterboice, walking along a narrow country road, I noticed a sign saying 'Honey for Sale' outside a lonely farmhouse. A jar of honey would be a pleasant addition to my frugal diet, I thought, and knocked at the door. There was no reply, so I walked around the house to see whether anybody was at the back. Yes, there at the far end of a long garden, under some apple trees, stood a man occupied with an assembly of traditional straw beehives. I approached slowly, only to freeze in my steps after a few yards, for I knew this man! Another few steps, and there could be no doubt. Shaking in my boots, I greeted him: 'Hello, Mr Schünemann!' It was his turn to be speechless, but Karl-Ernst burst out laughing; in order to avoid running into hordes of Berlin youngsters in the Scandinavian north, he had gone west this time, and had promptly been caught in the act by me! He took it gracefully, though; after all, we obviously had something in common, a predilection for honey, for instance. He too had stopped to buy some, and then, a former bee-keeper himself, had become fascinated by the old-fashioned hives. And now that we had bumped into each other, he suggested that I might as well stay with him for a while. He was stationed in Sligo, on Ballisadare Bay, trying to photograph the large seal colony there. However, bad weather in the west had sent him eastward to visit the Stone Age monuments in the Boyne valley. But back in Sligo, where I was heading anyway, I could be of assistance to him, rowing the boat, while he took photographs. I was only too delighted to accept the offer. So we left, still without honey, though I, for one, had received something far sweeter.

Like many children on the post-war Continent, I had grown up without a father or father-figure around. My father had died at the beginning of the war; my stepfather had died of his injuries a few days after it had ended. Whenever a friendly older male appeared in my world, my heart and mind would open up, looking for example and guidance. Karl-Ernst, at 33 years of age, was every young person's dream of a father or older brother, manly and firm, but also warm, caring and completely non-aggressive. Sitting beside him in his VW Beetle, I noted how closely he resembled the best-known images of Beethoven — the same energetic chin, mouth and forehead, the unruly hair, the overall proportions of the face — except that Beethoven's portraits always look grim, while Karl-Ernst's features, reflecting the many moods of every day, were predominantly on the bright side. I don't think he was aware of any similarity, and perhaps it was more a reflection of my own predisposition towards Beethoven, whose music had just begun to enthral me. But Karl-Ernst did sing, hum and whistle as we drove the lovely, empty roads of Ireland in the Fifties, and among all kinds of songs, themes from Beethoven's exuberant Eighth Symphony kept bubbling up, which seemed connected somehow with his fiancée, his 'sweet one', as he kept referring to her, who was due to arrive in Dublin in a week's time.

I myself, though, felt closer to the spirit of the Third, the 'Eroica', in Karl-Ernst's presence, that symphony dedicated to the 'memory of a great human being'. During those few days, I felt I was swept along on a wave of joyful activity. His goals were clear and open, at their core there was love for all things created, and a passionately and courageously held belief in their conservation. He shared readily from his own riches and thereby encouraged people to show their own best sides. Already he had made a number of good and reliable friends in Ireland; and everybody I later met who had known him also felt they had been touched by something extraordinary.

For me, the strongest visual memory of that extraordinariness comes from the night we spent in a 'Big House' in Collooney or Coolaney, I forget which. It was inhabited by a wiry, little old lady, some servants and a crowd of dogs. Karl-Ernst had made her acquaintance through their mutual interests in nature and archaeology and had a standing invitation to her home. When we arrived, unannounced, in the dark, there was a small dinner party in progress for an Anglo-Irish couple, a colonel with the beet-root face of an advanced alcoholic and his quiet wife. We were immediately asked to join the meal in the spacious dining-room, lit only by candles. The five of us were sitting around the large oval table, the lady and Karl-Ernst at the narrow ends, myself opposite the couple. The table was bright with linen and sparkling with silver and crystal, the centre-piece a large flower arrangement of deep-purple clematis and honey-coloured honeysuckle — the glowing colours and the sweet scent creating an effect that has epitomised for me ever since the idea of gracious living. The hitchhiker in me didn't know what was happening to him.

While we were being served, however, the colonel was getting more and more drunk and, to everyone's embarrassment, began delivering political and sexual innuendoes, the latter referring to me, the eighteen-year-old boy Karl-Ernst had picked up on the road. But Karl-Ernst kept his serenity throughout and, in his simple English, gave short, charming and disarming answers. He sat at his end of the table, his tanned face in repose, his blond hair aglow in the candlelight — a shining figure against the dark, like a portrait by Rembrandt. Getting up from the table, he was again beleaguered by the dogs of the house who had greeted him with mad excitement at our arrival. He had this effect on animals. Later I saw photographs of him taken during his time as a warden in Berlin's Zoological Garden, which showed him, a beaming Daniel in the lions' den, reclining on a heap of friendly big cats. On that evening, probably a little in love and immensely proud of him, I told myself never to forget these moments, these images, knowing I was in the presence of uncommon beauty.

The days that followed, however, were an anticlimax. We stayed on the shores of Ballisadare Bay, waiting. But a combination of unsuitable tides and miserable weather made the task for which I had been brought along impossible. A few forays ended in either mud or mist, and then it was time for Karl-Ernst to collect his 'sweet one' from Dublin airport and for me to continue on to Mayo, Connemara, the Midlands, and then back to Berlin, all the while carrying the memories of my encounter like a precious gift, an untouchable treasure.

Back in school I relished the envy of my classmates, their respect for a long journey successfully completed. We were all waiting for Karl-Ernst's reappearance in our school, with his slide-show about the seals of Ireland. Then my moment of quiet glory would come — after the show I would calmly approach him and, in front of the whole school, we would exchange experiences and memories of Ireland. I could hardly wait.

On the morning of the 28th of August 1957, on my way to school, I passed the newspaper-stand at our corner and, checking as usual the headlines of the popular *BILD Zeitung*, I found myself staring at the words: Berlin Zoo Photographer Missing Off Wales. My whole being told me immediately this had to be Karl-Ernst — as if my innermost fear was screaming there openly into my face. And he it was. After Ireland, he had crossed over to Skomer, for the large grey seal colony there. He had camped alone, as apart from him there were only two landscape painters on the island. When one evening he failed to arrive, as invited, for a meal with them, they searched for him and then raised the alarm. The autumn gales had arrived early that year, however, and atrocious weather held up the search. When it finally got underway, his pair of binoculars was discovered, at a seemingly innocuous spot. Nothing else was ever found of Karl-Ernst, not the slightest hint of what might have befallen him. The 'most beautiful summer of his life', as he had described it in a letter to his parents, had not let him go; the sea he had loved so much had claimed him for good.

It took me a long time to come to terms with his passing. I tried to tell myself that he had simply returned to the elements and could now be found in any natural setting, near the sea, especially, in the quiet surfacing of seals, in the swoops and shrieks of the terns, his favourite birds. We all know the limited success of such attempts at consolation, whereas time, in the end, does its work calmly and efficiently. Looking back now, I'm convinced that Ireland, too, was one of the losers in this tragedy. For Karl-Ernst was at the threshold of a great career in writing, in film and, most importantly, in television. He had charisma, passion and already enormous experience. He had loved Ireland and his photographs, which I later saw, would have made a huge impression in Germany. His book on Ireland would have illustrated the country Heinrich Böll described in his *Irish Diary* and would most likely have caused an even greater influx of German visitors to this country. And, who knows, the country itself might earlier have become more conscious and more caring about its natural heritage. He would have made a difference.

And that's why the entry on Skomer in the aforementioned book gave me such a jolt: Seal Cove — was this the place that had witnessed Karl-Ernst's last moments? And had the treacherous surface of the island, that 'tissue of fragility', anything to do with his disappearance? But apart from such speculations, there arose in me a surge of beautiful music from the depth of my memory where it had settled quietly over the years, a man transfigured into a symphony, complete with his 'Marcia Funebre'. For the final chords of this music I have to call on the very last words in Karl-Ernst's book on the sea-eagles of Norway, which appeared posthumously. After having spent a whole summer living with them, he sees, on the day of his departure, a group of six eagles heading southwards: 'Longingly I followed them with my eyes,

wishing that I too could fly like them over land and sea —
boundless!'

My First Fresh Fig

I had my first fresh fig not from the fruit-stand in a supermarket nor in one of the countries where fig-trees grow naturally, but in Ireland, more than 40 years ago, in a farmyard, and in somewhat delicate circumstances.

I was touring Ireland then on my own, my knapsack on my back, and had just visited the monumental dolmen at Browne's Hill, near Carlow Town, when I was addressed by a woman standing at a farm-gate. As it was about lunch-time, an invitation for a cup of tea soon followed. That was quite normal then. There were five children in the family, the older three were girls of around my own age, 16, 18 and 19 respectively; to my eyes they were all three unbelievably pretty. And to them too I must have appeared like a godsend: a nice, dark-haired foreigner, with bare, brown legs and a natural ease with girls because of a different cultural background, who had been dropped, out of the blue of a boring country summer day, straight into the lap of their family — had, in fact, been introduced to them by their own mother.

Nature immediately set about taking its course. Eileen, the youngest of the three, took possession of the boy, with the straightforwardness of a child and the physical aplomb of a young woman; I can still hear her screams of triumph and delight as I carried her, under her orders, on my shoulders around the farmyard, and her shrieks of terror when I threatened to throw her off. She steered me to an old beech-tree and made me cut our initials into the bark. I obliged, of course, but I also made sure that Mary, the girl my own age, 18, was aware whose name I would really have liked to carve. For I soon realised it was she my heart went out to, she was quiet and gentle and mysterious in her comings and goings, it was not easy to keep track of her and convey my eye-message. But convey it I did, and felt sure that I got the desired response.

Margaret, the oldest, stayed in the background, waiting for her moment to pounce. It seemed to come later that evening when she had to leave for work in the local pub and invited me for a pint — she knew the way to a man's heart. But Eileen would not let me out of her grasp, nor was I prepared to lose sight of Mary.

The evening also brought a jubilant announcement: tomorrow, Saturday, both parents would leave for the weekend to attend a distant wedding, but I would of course stay and we would all have a wonderful party! I was a bit overawed by the prospect, but also, who would blame me, thoroughly intrigued. Later in the evening we all assembled around the fireplace. At this stage I felt already like one of the family. I played a bit on my mouth-organ, and then they called on Eileen to sing. And sing she did! Ladies of *A Woman's Heart* — eat your hearts out, none of you can sing like Eileen Conroy sang on that night! She had a natural, strong, golden-coloured alto, and she sang from the fullness of her young years. As her voice soared, we in that yellow-painted, fire-flickering room soared with her. 'This is My Island in the

Sun' was one of the songs she sang, and my heart glowed in passionate agreement.

I slept little the rest of that night on a mattress in the kitchen and, I suppose, was not the only one whose mind was wild with imaginings. The next morning Mrs Conroy took me quietly aside and said that while I was a nice boy, and they all liked me very much, unfortunately I couldn't stay any longer. Her husband gave me a generous lift in the direction of Dublin — and thus our weekend joined the realm of What-Might-Have-Been, the very home-ground of our romantic lives. The girls soon afterwards all went to Glasgow to work as waitresses and factory-hands; Mary and I corresponded for a while, but then her letters trickled out.

So, what about that fresh fig then? Oh yes — that fig. Sometime in the course of that sunny, turbulent afternoon, I overheard Eileen and Mary crossing words: 'Yes, why not?' 'Oh no, we mustn't!' 'Ah, come on!' — in the end, the yesses won out, and the two of them led me into the overgrown back garden which was surrounded by high walls — there was long grass everywhere, soggy patches and clumps of nettles which stung my bare legs. Finally we arrived in a secluded, sunny corner where a fig-tree grew up the wall, bearing one plump, ripe fruit. Without saying a word, Mary picked and presented it to me. With a supremely masculine gesture I took out my pocket-knife, sliced it in two and offered each of them half. Oh no, it was all for me! I stood there, looking down on the two dark-red, glistening surfaces in my palms, and then, for the first time in my life, savoured the strange, earthy, metallic taste of a fresh fig. The girls watched me silently, one smiling, the other not. And then we trod back, slightly trembling and benumbed, back to the open, unconfusing spaces of the front farmyard.

Defeat and After

For a couple of years the drama group in our West Berlin school was blessed with two protagonists who, equally talented, complemented each other perfectly. Klaus Hoffmann was blond and freckled; his square face with pale blue eyes often showed a thin, impish grin; his stout body seemed to work like a magnet on his arms — only the most necessary, most incisive gestures would escape. His stage presence was magisterial, thanks mainly to his prime asset, a glorious bass voice, warm, sandy, with an edge, and well-controlled. A voice is one thing, though; you also need the mind to do something with it, and Klaus's mind was bright as well as naturally mature; in fact, you could only imagine him having been born mature and dignified, and crying, if he ever did, in a soothing bass voice.

Having thus presented Klaus in some detail saves me the embarrassment of having to describe the other pillar of our group, namely myself, other than saying that I was, in almost every sense, his opposite — dark-haired, romantic and gesticulating. And naturally immature. No wonder we were regularly cast as opponents on the stage, typically in father-and-son situations, which was not without a touch of irony as Klaus was my junior by at least a year. There would be precious few parts where a director would have to think twice before choosing between the two of us. But on one occasion we were competitors, head to head, mind to mind and voice to voice.

Our group was also involved in regular literary morning services in the school's assembly hall, the texts of the readings usually selected from the works of Hermann Hesse, after whom the school was named. Normally we were assigned certain texts and simply accepted them, but on this occasion Klaus was to recite a particular poem which meant a lot to me, and I mentioned that. No problem, I was told, for our next rehearsal Klaus and I should prepare ourselves to audition for the poem, and then a vote would follow. Fine — I felt I had already half-won my case.

The poem, by Hermann Hesse, was titled 'Idle Thoughts', but as so often when things are declared 'idle', they are anything but. Written in 1940, the poem shows Hesse's despair and revulsion at yet another European war. Each of the four stanzas is in a starkly contrasting mood. The first predicts a final end to these 'foolishly ingenious' wars, when nothing will be left on earth but the natural world, human history, mankind itself having been extinguished and forgotten. And forgotten as well would be all the beautiful things: children's play, languages, music — 'everything that our loving has inscribed into the willing Earth'. Earth will have no light anymore. The last stanza brings in the Creator who had watched with equanimity the end of 'all the horrible and all the lovely'. He looks at the liberated planet as it hovers darkly amidst the sparkling stars. Pensively He grasps a handful of clay and, once again, begins giving it shape ...

I must have been around 18 then, and the poem expressed my own feelings towards the flawed species I found myself belonging to — emotions dithering between hope and despair, pity and contempt. I also harboured my first doubts about the Creator's benevolence towards, or even interest in, His creation. But the real satisfaction lay not in finding my own, vague enough, feelings expressed in the poem, but in finding them expressed so beautifully: the grim firmness of the phrasing, the soulful fall of the lines, the intricate but unlaboured finality of the rhymes. In short: I had been hit by a work of art. Here was a form into which I could pour my shapelessness. And so I prepared myself carefully for our joust, feeling confident.

In the event, there was hardly a contest. I put into my recitation all I had — which was too much. Klaus gave the measured, newsreader delivery I had expected and had wanted to counteract. The vote was clearly in his favour and, to be honest, I couldn't argue with it. His interpretation, if it was one, was objective, and objectivity, in matters of art, is an indisputable quality.

Nevertheless — I had lost when and where it counted, and I felt absolutely vanquished. But, strangely, not weakened, not discouraged. Rather the opposite: a surprisingly nourishing, forward-looking stubbornness arose in me out of my failure, a conviction that I had found what gave me the greatest satisfaction, perhaps even a sense of direction. Or had it found me? Was it even a calling? If so, a very small one, nothing to boast about. But there could be no question of ever letting my discovery slip away again. Instead, I continued doing that which brought with it the joys of self-discovery time and again — serving the word, the poetic word, with the limited means at my command — voice, insight, imagination. Reading and reciting poems or stories became the red thread that has run through my entire life, perhaps even kept it from unravelling. The ball of thread left in my hands is small by now, and if I could wrap it all up again, it would lead me back through the maze of my life, through all the rooms I have been in as a word-worker — stages of all sizes, studios of several kinds, classrooms and lecture halls, bar-rooms and bedrooms, the poetry-translator's torture-chamber and the quiet room of disquiet which the poet inhabits. The thread even helped me across the gulf between two countries, two cultures. And if I were to follow it all the way back to the beginning, I would finally arrive at the entrance to my private labyrinth and find the thread slung there around a standing stone — the memorial to a most necessary defeat over some anything but idle thoughts.

To the Brandenburg Gate!

For two weeks in late autumn of 1956 the world was captivated by the momentous events in Hungary; we in Berlin were glued to our radios, to the incoming reports which followed, with a sickening inevitability, the pattern of what we had experienced in the heart of our own city only three years ago; again the initial flourishing of a popular rebellion was soon to be eclipsed and crushed by the might of Soviet tanks. Our own barely closed wounds were torn open again. The transmissions from the last hours of the uprising — those ever more urgent, more desperate appeals for Help! Help! from the West — help that had been half-promised in the beginning! — the shooting that could be heard in the background of those fearful, pleading, proud voices, the silence after the radio station had been taken — these sounds burnt themselves into our minds and memories forever. Was there nothing we in West Berlin could do? No, there wasn't; in fact our own situation was as precarious as that of the Hungarians, and we could easily be next on the Soviet list. Still, our impotent rage needed some form or forum of expression and, as was by now traditional in times of crisis, the city fathers called a mass meeting.

I was among the crowd of more than 100,000 Berliners, a 17-year-old who was only just beginning the long process of awakening to reality. The people around me were grim with anger and despair and in dire need of hearing words of empathy, of direction. But on this occasion speaker after speaker failed to come up with just such words, which they probably couldn't find in their own minds. The sounds of discontent, of unreleased frustration, were increasing, and the mood was becoming volatile. Then, out of the blue, in the middle of a particularly uninspired address, the speaker suddenly shouted just three words, yet they worked like the proverbial spark in the powder-keg: '*Zum Brandenburger Tor!*' A guttural roar of approval rose and, as one man, the crowd turned and moved, nay, stormed in the direction of the Gate. It was only next day that we learned how an anonymous young man, impatient with the speaker, had pushed him aside to shout those three words into the microphone.

I was in the middle of that surging crowd, swept along willingly, for the first and last time in my life, lustfully experiencing the sensation of being just one particle in a torrent of communal emotion, of being, for once, undistanced from my people. The approach to the Gate, about two miles, took some steam out of us, but our numbers were augmented by people on the streets who heard what was going on and spontaneously joined us. I was running along on light feet, running was my natural rhythm, but gradually my rational mind was reasserting itself. What would we do, once at the Gate, then still a working border check-point? March through it? Climb on it? Stand there and shout? There was no rational core to what we were doing. So many years later I'm still amazed at the almost religious, mystical belief we must have had in the power of the monument to work a miracle, to deliver us from our distress, and the world from evil. Soon I found myself at the margin of the main column of marchers, more an observer now than a fiery participant.

It didn't take us long, it seemed, before we arrived in the Tiergarten, at the other end of which the Gate was waiting. On the 'Street of the 17th of June', named after the failed uprising in East Germany in 1953, our advance was stopped by a cordon of West Berlin police. We were confused. Hadn't we been officially sent out on this sortie, only to be called back now by the same people? First roused, then hampered? There was pushing, shoving and shouting from the crowd, as the police appealed for calm, vainly. I turned away from the scene and saw it would be no problem to circumvent the cordon by simply breaking up into smaller groups and making our way through the darkness of the parkland. So far only the road was blocked. I kept my knowledge to myself, though, and was glad the masses preferred staying together and ramming their heads against the obstacle at hand, our own police force. More and more people arrived and were pushing from the back, new shouts of 'To the Brandenburg Gate!' arose, and the situation looked about to become explosive. Then, when it really seemed as if the cordon would have to give or violence would break out, a voice was heard, from a hand-held megaphone, which made everybody pause and listen.

Willy Brandt was at that time only the Speaker of Berlin's House of Parliament, and had not been one of the platform speakers at the rally. It was obvious though to everybody that he was the coming man. Much later, as Federal Chancellor, he would fall on his knees in front of the Monument to the Ghetto Uprising in Warsaw, a politician with a firm sense of honour, and of shame, and for the meaningful, symbolic gesture. It turned out he had been rushed to the scene in the

Tiergarten, and here, too, he had a fine hour. The crowd was soon spellbound by his energetic, passionately rational language; a man incapable of platitudes, he found the words they had hungered for, making clear what was possible in our situation and what was definitely not. The people fell silent, if not appeased then at least brought to their senses, until the protest ended with a heartfelt rendering of '*Ich hatt einen Kameraden*', a song traditionally sung in memory of fallen soldiers. And then we made our different ways home, empty, sobered and sad. Brandt later commented on the events of this night in his autobiography, remarking dryly that it is always useful to remember that one's fellow countrymen are fond of singing.

In that way, a night that could have ended in a bloodbath ended with a song. Unbeknownst to us, tanks and machine-guns had already been positioned on the eastern side of the Gate, a clash there could have had catastrophic consequences. The papers next day claimed that Brandt had prevented the outbreak of World War III. That may or may not have been the case — nobody can tell — but he certainly had won a victory for patience and reason, one that in the East-West context pointed far, far into the future. And as for the people at that rally, including myself, we can tell ourselves that at least once in our lifetimes we were physically present at an historical event, where we had witnessed at first hand the inextricable interplay between the powers of the one and the force of the many. And where the great achievement of the one had been to make something momentous *not* happen.

Figures on an Altar

The visitor to the German city of Würzburg will repeatedly come across the names of two men there. One is St Kilian, an Irish missionary monk who brought Christianity to the region, in gratitude for which the locals chopped off his head. Eight hundred years later, the bearer of the second name, Tilman Riemenschneider, barely escaped a similar fate for taking the wrong side, that of the losers, in the Peasants' Revolts of the early 16th century. As he was one of the most renowned artists of the time, his death would have been a loss for all sides, and so he got away with incarceration. Today his wood and stone sculptures are considered to epitomise late medieval art, and they can still be seen in many churches and chapels throughout the region, making him as synonymous with it as is St Kilian, Apostle of Franconia, the monk from Ireland.

When I was in my late teens, I was smitten by Riemenschneider, to the extent of making my own pilgrimage, on foot, to as many places with his statues as I could reach. It's difficult, half a lifetime later, to explain this obsession, even to myself. But I think I learned to read the human face from him, the alphabet, the initial grounding. His men and women appeared to be so 'modern', a word which in those years was to me expressive not only of despair and doubt but also of a quiet and dignified resignation to being conscious and alone in a cruel world. All of this seemed to me to be almost paradoxical in the wholly Christian context of these altarpieces, on themes such as the Ascension of the Virgin, the Last Supper and, of course, the Crucifixion.

Today I suspect I projected the frailty of my own faith into these saintly figures, with their visionary, wide-open eyes, their melancholy but composed features as, after a day's hike through the sweltering heat of the summer of 1959, I finally sat in the restful coolness of one of those little churches, staring, breathing, allowing their silent presence to seep into mine. That was my way, then, of trying to get close to their maker's mind — and on one occasion it looked as if I might truly succeed.

The sacristan of one of the churches had noticed my persistence and mentioned the name of a village where one could see a little-known work by Riemenschneider, well worth a visit. So I set out for the place, called Wettringen, arriving there after walking for half a day. The church, which turned out to be a Protestant one, was closed. But the minister's house was nearby, so I knocked. He opened the door himself, a tall, young, enthusiastic man. He was busy at the moment, but got the key nevertheless and strode ahead. The church was cool and bare, and above the altar stood a crucifixion group, every one of the five or six figures bearing the stylistic hallmarks of the workshop of Riemenschneider. My guide proudly pointed out some details, as I began withdrawing into my habitual staring silence. He had to go then, but left the key with me, and also made a strange remark which took me by surprise. If I felt like touching the figures, I shouldn't hesitate to climb up onto the altar, he said with an encouraging nod. And then he was gone, and I was on my own.

I was amazed, what a gift of trust he had bestowed on me, a complete stranger! And no, I didn't really have the desire to touch the sculptures, I was quite happy just looking at them. But then, slowly, the idea of actually feeling their substance grew ever more tempting. As a former altar-boy, though, I first had to overcome a natural inhibition before I put my hands on the altar and lifted myself up. It was covered with white linen, and I had to be careful to keep my boots away from it. Uneasily kneeling, struggling not to lose my balance, I straightened up, and raised my hands to the dark figures. And let my fingers glide over them, first with my eyes open, and then closed. It felt like — wood, hard, dry wood. A papery, parchment-like surface, like a cocoon — I remember that image crossing my mind. That was all. No more fundamental experience, insight or even revelation. Sobered, but also vaguely relieved, I climbed down and reverted to my contemplative stare. If the eyes don't have it, I thought, the touch won't do it. And doubted even the doubting Thomas.

So — had I really come closer to the troubled and ambivalent mind of Riemenschneider as I knelt on that altar, holding his creations in my hands? It doesn't look like it. Maybe closer to my own mind, and to its major failing, that of being forever dominated by the surface of existing things. On that day, I simply handed back the key and continued my wanderings through the summery landscape of Franconia, shimmering with heat, and wheat and dust.

Unfair Competition

During one summer, as a student, I worked a seven-day week. Weekdays I was on a building site, cleaning and repainting the metal substructure of the Berlin Underground where it runs overground; it was primitive, physically demanding and dirty work, drawing only men from the bottom drawer of the labour force, plus me. On weekends, however, I moved in nobler circles; I was a museum guard, wearing a dark suit. I had been hand-picked by Dr Reidemeister himself, the Generaldirektor of Berlin's State Museums, a tall and intimidating Prussian gentleman who had put me through a stern interview before assigning me to a truly exceptional exhibition; the famous Bührle Collection of French Impressionists, containing some of the best-known paintings of the period, was to come to Berlin as a special favour from Bührle, who was an arms manufacturer and made a lot of money from the Cold War, in which Berlin, of course, was the lynch-pin.

My job was clearly defined: if any hand got closer than, say, ten inches to the surface of a painting, I was to intervene. Now should anybody think this kind of work is easy, all I can say is that, by Sunday evenings, I was looking forward to the next morning on the building site. Standing for eight hours in overcrowded, badly ventilated rooms with practically nothing to do, because 99.99 per cent of people don't touch pictures in museums, is not just back-breaking, it is terminally boring.

The pictures don't really compensate, not for eight hours anyway.

In that situation what will a young man of 20 do in order to distract, entertain and reward himself? But of course, while they feasted their eyes on the Impressionists, I, impressionable and romantically inclined as I was, feasted mine on the charms of our lady visitors. Until one Saturday afternoon I had an apparition — the most enchantingly feminine creature my eyes had as yet been blessed with! A walking brightness, blonde, willowy, tastefully dressed, her face shining with inner contentment — she, looking at pictures, was a sight to be seen.

In moments like these I had an arrangement with my elderly colleagues, who would swap rooms so that I could follow the beauty in question through the entire exhibition. That's what we did on that day. Wherever *she* was, I was too, just standing there, admiring. After a while, and a couple of rooms, she noticed, and the sweetest, most gratifying smile stole over her face: she appreciated my appreciation! Not to be unmannerly, I then backed off, but when she left, I was there again, and I didn't deceive myself! There was that smile again, and a barely perceptible nod before the door closed behind her. I knew, I just knew, I would see her again.

And I did. The next morning, Sunday, when there were as yet not many visitors, the door opened and there she was, more radiant than the evening before. And with her came the boss, Dr Reidemeister, and a third person, one with a very well-known face indeed: Herbert von Karajan, chief conductor of the Berlin Philharmonic, the busiest man in the world, had made time to look at paintings his newly betrothed had enthused about. Yes, now I remembered, I had seen her face before, on photographs of von Karajan's engagement to Eliette, a French model. Much had been made in the papers of the age difference, he had just turned 50, she was only 20 — my own age!

Now he entered the place with the aplomb of one who is used to spontaneous applause on his appearance. And poor, mighty Reidemeister was so unhappy about his height! In order to grovel properly, he had to bend down to the rather small great man who granted him his ear, with its famous perfect pitch, and, without looking at the museum's director, nodded knowingly to his explanations. Reidemeister was gesticulating a lot and came rather too close to the pictures, but did we intervene? You must be joking! Eliette today had eyes only for her man — and it had to be admitted, he was impressive, bestriding our exhibition as if the stately wing of Charlottenburg Palace was just an adjunct to his worldwide empire. And Eliette his chosen empress.

I was terribly, terribly embarrassed. Why did I feel embarrassed? I hadn't done anything wrong, trespassed or interfered. But out of some ancient, primitive instinct, I drew back, and the reverse arrangement to yesterday's room-swapping came into play: wherever those three were, I was not.

Forty years have since passed. Eliette is a widow now. I really must try and get her telephone number. I'm sure she remembers me.

Part II

First Station

On Thin Ice

Nobody would have said they were meant for each other. Certainly they themselves didn't, not for a good while. To begin with, they were of a rather similar type, dark-haired and romantic, and of the same height, so that the girl appeared taller. They were sometimes taken to be brother and sister, and that was, more or less, how they felt themselves, initially. But they did have things in common which separated them from the 20 or so other students of their class in the school of acting. Social and cultural background, for instance, which for both of them was humble and, accompanying it, a way of presenting themselves which lacked assuredness. They were, and would remain, at the fringe of their class. Age, too, played a part. The girl, at 18, was the youngest of them all and, despite her dramatic, brooding looks, not yet quite hatched from the shell of childhood — a combination which the boy, who was two years older, found ever more intriguing. He had just the right amount of reading, travelling and loving behind him to make him acceptable to a girl who, having grown up with an abusive, alcoholic father, had taken an early vow to revenge herself and her mother on the rest of men. They soon discovered they came from the same remote district of Berlin and so spent many hours commuting in the Underground, facing each other, more and more aware. Clearly, for all her aloofness, she was also in need of tenderness — perhaps even in need of giving it — so he fortified himself with patience and felt his attachment grow, even in the times of maddening jealousy she quite deliberately set out to kindle in him.

Their teachers had very different approaches. One of them placed the greatest emphasis on word-perfectness, and not just the words but punctuation too. A full stop, for instance, was just that, a stop in a rush forward, a stepping-stone for crossing a current of argument or passion. A chance also to take a breath, such a precious commodity. Their task as actors, she said, was to find their breath in the breath of the people they were portraying: breath was the river that would carry them along. Commas, too, were breath-marks, occasions to take one's bearings, to take aim again. Oh, and dashes — moments of hesitation or confusion or, at the end of a sentence, sighs, doubts, a fading into speechlessness. Not to mention the importance of a question mark, the awesome stage-potential of the exclamation mark! But words, dots and strokes were just the surface, the outward signs of what lay hidden beneath — the whole physical reality of their parts. That they had to bring to life — an undertaking not without risks, and requiring courage.

The room where the two were rehearsing their scenes, one of many for that purpose in the building, was a small, vault-like chamber in the basement, sparsely furnished with just a table and a few chairs, with little light from the one small window. Here they met, drawn more and more irresistibly to their meetings, where, naturally, the borderline between literature and their lives became ever more blurred. The scenes they worked on were from the classical repertoire, mostly love scenes. They did study their words, including the punctuation, but simultaneously they learned of the wondrous abilities of their bodies to feel and to make feel. Uninformed and shy as they were, it took them many months before they arrived in the definitively sexual sphere, but well before that they had made the most bewildering discoveries about hitherto quite innocuous parts of their bodies: palms, wrists, the crook of an elbow, the details of a knee. As in their texts, an infinity of requisite research and contemplation was opening up, punctuated by full stops and deep breaths, doubts and sighs, entangled with awakening glances and the movements of alerted limbs. Not to mention whispered questions and unsupressable exclamations.

Sometimes when the room became too heated, their closeness cloying, they fled from it. Like the time in midwinter when they crossed the road and ran into the forest, with its clean, powdery cloak of new snow. The orange trunks of the pine trees stood out glowing against the frosty blue of the sky. Snow-loads slipped now and then from the dark branches, and then a myriad diamonds drifted through the bright air. They followed an elongated lake that wound its way between the sandy hills. Having escaped the frightening intimacy of their erotic cave, the two now frolicked in the sudden freedom of their togetherness, chasing each other and allowing themselves to be caught, seeing the plumes of their breath mingle and separate as they walked arm in arm.

The sun was sinking low when they suddenly realised that they had forgotten the time — they wouldn't make it for their acting class if they continued their walk around the lake. That was unthinkable, their teacher as much a stickler for punctuality as she was for punctuation. But, hey, the solution to their problem lay before their eyes — the frozen surface of the lake! Crossing it would make the difference. Their hearts beat faster. There was nobody around. Was this a gamble? It had been freezing for many days now, the ice near the shore was rock-solid. Their decision was quick and mutual. Initially their steps rang out on compact, smooth, milky-white ice, but soon the surface became rippled, like sea-sand at low tide, as if the water had frozen the moment a breeze had ruffled it. As they approached the middle of the lake, the ice under their feet turned clearer and clearer; at first there were still air-bubbles enclosed in it, but then it became as transparent as water. They could see straight down into the depths below them, a greenish-black abyss, as if they were walking on invisible glass. Presently, thin white lines spread across the surface from under their feet, accompanied by a faint, crackling noise. They were now at the centre of the lake; to stop now, with the weight of their two bodies so close together, would be suicide. The only way was forward. With just a word or two — from whom? — they let go of their hands and ran ahead, at an angle. And would have run straight into calamity if, just as on the other side, the ice hadn't turned ripply, and milky, and firm again, until it rang out under their heels like steel. Finally, again, the hard, frozen earth. They had made it, separately. They looked at each other, both of them shaking. Then, moving slowly, they grabbed and held on to each other, breathing, breathing. What had they done? What were they doing?

In Dark Times

Surely we're all sometimes puzzled about first experiences —
the first friendship, the first trip to a foreign country, the first
book, the first kiss, of course, the first corpse. And all the
other firsts life is full of, even at an advanced age. How did
they come about, and what did they set in motion? And so,
looking back, even lives which sometimes seem quite
shapeless can acquire what looks like structure, even
consequence and necessity.

My first role as a professional actor came my way when I
was still in the school of acting in Berlin. It was the part of the
narrator in a play that had already been running for years in
the city's only fringe theatre then, the *Vaganten* (the
Travellers). The title of the play was *Dr Korczak and the
Children*.

Now, the name Janusz Korczak may not mean anything in
Ireland, but on the Continent and especially in Poland and
Germany it is well-known in the world of education. Born in
1878, Korczak was a Polish paediatrician, educational theorist
and author of children's books. Central to his thinking was his
conviction of the absolute right of every child to be respected
— which may sound trivial in our enlightened times, but
certainly was not so a hundred years ago. During the German
occupation of Poland, Janusz Korczak headed a Jewish home
for orphans and homeless children in the Warsaw Ghetto.

When, in August 1942, the children, 200 of them, were to be transported to Treblinka, Korczak, because of his international standing, was given the option to escape. He refused. Seeing the inevitability of his children's fate he wanted to reassure them through his presence for as long as possible. And so he accompanied them to Treblinka and led them, singing, into the gas chamber.

That is the story of *Dr Korczak and the Children* — the noblest and the lowest that mankind can find in itself, face to face. The play deals with its almost unbearable theme in a Pirandelloesque manner — actors stepping out of their roles, introducing private attitudes into their acting parts, thus giving the audience moments of respite, before dragging them even deeper into the action. There were only five of us in the cast, one a child. No costumes, almost no props or stage-set. We could perform the piece practically anywhere, and we did in those winter months of 1960-61, when Berlin, at least culturally, was still one city. We travelled to the remotest corners, especially of East Berlin, playing in schools, old-age homes, community halls and hospitals. I remember it as a dark, dank time; the difference between East and West Berlin was marked, it was the year of the building of the Wall. We drove along endless, badly lit suburban streets, many venues were in a poor state, dim and barely heated. Sometimes, in tiny rooms, we stepped on people's toes, at other times we had to call out to an invisible audience at the back of some cavernous community hall. Silent audiences. When we got no applause, or just one feeble round, we knew we had done our job well.

Our last performance was at a venue which filled us all with trepidation if not fear — the theatre-hall in the Jewish

Community Centre in West Berlin. Was it right for us, non-Jewish actors, to come to such a place and act out on stage events our audience was all too horribly familiar with in real life? But we had been invited, and so we went, apprehensive and in a spirit of expiation.

The stage turned out to be so huge we felt lost on it, with our few things to hold on to, and our words. With the glaring spotlights on us, we were dwarfed in every sense, and utterly bare. There was only a handful of people in the large auditorium. When my final speech came — the Prophet Ezekiel's vision of an entire field of white, human bones, all putting on flesh again, culminating with the words: 'Thus sayeth the Lord: Behold, O my people, I will open your graves, and call you to come up out of your graves, and you shall live, and I shall bring you into the land of Israel' — I tried to dig as deeply as possible into my 20 years of inexperience, but all I can remember now is my voice echoing, as voices do in vast, empty spaces.

Afterwards we met some of the few spectators we'd had — small, withered, elderly people who shook our hands in silence and looked into our faces with pained, tearless eyes, nodding, just nodding at us.

In Our Lord's Valley

Our Lord's Valley, the *Herrgottstal,* is in the region of Franconia in North Bavaria, not far from the picturesque, medieval town of Rothenburg ob der Tauber. After a farmer in the Middle Ages found a sacred wafer in his field, the chapel built on the spot became a place of pilgrimage and, in 1510, acquired an altarpiece by the great sculptor Tilman Riemenschneider, the best preserved and most ethereal of his surviving works. Its centre-piece is the 'Assumption of the Virgin' — the aged Mary, who has witnessed her Son's death on the cross, is shown as young again, the girl she was before all that had happened to her. Below her, two groups of apostles huddle together, their faces showing signs of age and grief, of doubt and earthly suffering, as they lift them to the young girl who is about to rise beyond their imagination.

Today the chapel is a major tourist attraction in the area; when we visited it, in August 1961, you didn't even have to pay to get in and, during the few days we spent in a guest-house next door, we used to drop in whenever we passed by, to sit down for a while and try to open our minds to what we saw. We were on holiday there, my love and I, and it was in that guest-house we shared, for the first time, one room and one bed. It was called *Zum Stier* (The Bull), after the name of the owner, who was also the local butcher. Bullish also described the physical appearance of the owner, but we only

76

saw him in fleeting moments. His wife, an equally robust woman, at least physically, had been very kind to the clearly unmarried couple, all of 22 and 19 years of age respectively, who had tentatively asked for a double room. With a friendly, understanding smile she had led us to an upstairs room with a wide bedstead, the eiderdowns two bulging hills, the white linen, shimmering pillows waiting to receive my love's long, raven-black hair. We were hesitant lovers, but innocent, in the religious sense of the images in the chapel next door, we weren't anymore. But as we roamed the summery, pastoral landscape, as yet undesecrated by pylons, transmitters and the car culture, we felt at times part of another innocence, an older, less narrowly defined one.

On our outings, the dogs of the *Stier* were our enthusiastic companions. We were young and strong, and driven by a wonderful, almost inexhaustible restlessness; we ran most of the time, which was what the dogs wanted; they were happy. In between, during short breaks, we lay side by side on the crest of some hill, catching our breath, talking, laughing. And the dogs, with their beaming faces, were near us. We were lightly clad in the midsummer heat, our bodies, so intimately known to each other by now, yet still so mysterious, lay in parallel harmony, their lines merging with those of the slopes and groves of Our Lord's Valley. In quiet rapture I looked at my love's beautiful Grecian profile, her dark eyes fixed on the heat-hazy horizon. Such must have been the gods of antiquity, I thought, eternally young, roaming the classical landscape at will, now invisible, now materialising into shining entities, loving, hunting, speeding thought-like wherever they wished, at one with the world. Had it not been for our eager, but short-legged little dachshunds holding us back, we ourselves might have grown wings at our heels and taken to the air.

Our first night in the Stier's Inn was disturbed by a strange noise that rolled down the valley in repeated, rumbling thunderclaps. Next morning we discovered the source: a bowling-alley, by its appearance as old as the Riemenschneider altarpiece, stretched deep in the inn's backgarden. There was just a single lane, sheltered by a long, rickety, red-tiled roof. The wooden surface of the lane was warped, the bowling balls from decades or centuries of use worn and odd-shaped, the pins battered into pitiable shapes. We rolled a few balls, the ensuing noise reminding my love of a German fairy tale where the devil plays skittles with human skulls and bones.

And the next night, too, brought with it noise and fear. As we were, at last, sinking back into our mountainous eiderdowns, we were startled by an awful roar: this time from the massive chest of our host, the Stier, frightening, volcanic sounds, as his mighty bulk bounced against doors and furniture, threatening to demolish the entire ground floor. From his wife we only heard a few sharp, subdued words. Then followed a series of hard slaps which gradually turned the Stier's roar into a howl. My love was trembling. I got up, cautiously opened our door and looked down from the landing. There, in the hall, stood the woman of the house, bringing down, with all her strength, a sturdy stick on the fleshy back of her husband, the drunk, the way people sometimes hit stubborn animals. Her face was calm, hard and very sad. I slipped back into our bed where my love, the huntress of the day, made herself as small as she could, whimpering, hiding in the hollow of my body for protection

— I only had an inkling, then, of the childhood memories that were flooding her frightened mind at that moment. I hummed low, reassuring sounds, while outside in the night, the Stier begged for mercy, the blows raining down hurting both him and his wife. In the bowling alley behind the house, the devil threw human skulls after human bones, Our Lord's Valley echoed with earthly thunder, and in the chapel next door 12 anxious men clung to their books, their faces raised to a young girl, pleading for her intercession.

The Duels in *Hamlet*

My first boss was a fierce creature, and he looked it: bald head, grey skin, tufts of grizzly hair standing out from above his hairy ears, long face, long nose, long, yellow teeth between scant lips, eyebrows askew like whiskers over deeply set grey eyes — yes, the face of a wolf, nothing less. His body was short and lean, his movements were forceful but jerky, his energy ferocious; if you had to move in his proximity it was impossible to evade the knocks from his bony limbs, striking out in all directions. He was the centre of a circle of fear which he was anxious to feed from within. Over many years of managing theatres, in East Prussia and Latvia among other places, he had got used to ordering people around, and now I was his main daily target. My beginner's contract combined the duties of actor and director's assistant. As a young actor you were of little importance in the German theatres of the early Sixties; as a director's assistant you were even less, the lowest life form in the house. At the same time you had a very responsible job, for as they say, if anything went wrong, you were responsible.

One summer he tried his hand on a production of *Hamlet*, on an open-air stage, the hedge theatre in the beautiful royal gardens of Herrenhausen, in Hannover. That alone, if you ask me, was a daft idea; if there is any place in the world that is not spooky, it's those formally laid out, strictly symmetrical baroque gardens. Technology, however, was to come to our aid: when Hamlet urges Horatio and the soldiers not to tell anybody what they have heard and seen, his father's ghost, from under the stage-floor, commands them to SWEAR! And those ghostly orders were to come, thunderously, from a number of loudspeakers hidden in the hedges, as our earthen stage, of course, was not hollow underneath.

Now the boss and I were in the studio to record the ghost's voice which the boss himself would supply. It was late in the evening, after a long day of rehearsals. I was exhausted but he was in his element, crouching behind the microphone and hollering SWEAEAHAHAR! with a howling, hollow vibrato. He had it played back to him, and then did it again: SWEAEAHAHAR! That went on and on. It was awful. Within me rose a desperate, terrible fury. When he finally strutted out to us, looking very pleased with himself and waiting for our compliments, I lost my temper and snapped at him: 'That was completely wrong! The king has given orders all his life, why should he now, after death, sound like the ghost in a pantomime?' The tone of supreme authority coming from my mouth shocked even myself. He stood in front of me, hands trembling, his body leaning forward, breathing heavily. It looked as if he was about to leap at my throat. I held his glance however and felt my words working in him. What appealed to him, I think, was the idea of undiminished authority even after the final exit from the world of the living. So, rather than strangling me, he suddenly swivelled around, rushed back to the mike, barked an authoritative SWEAR! and stormed out, with me in tow, full of foreboding.

Justifiably so, as it turned out. The dress rehearsal was a sham. Our futuristic attempts at *Quadrophenia* failed miserably. I quickly realised that there was no hope of the sound effects working, not in the available time, with the equipment at hand and an elderly sound engineer overwhelmed by the task and subject to fits of panic. Hamlet, a big star of the time, made his displeasure known. Not surprisingly, my name rang out as I was summoned in apoplectic tones.

I walked out onto the vacated stage, all lights on me, slim, small and shrinking. The show trial was to begin, the backlash of yesterday's transgression. I can still feel the moment in my bones: I was exquisitely on my own and that — 'take it for all in all' — was not a bad thing. His voice stabbed at me from out of the blinding darkness: 'Will — this — ever — work?' The moment of truth. I took a deep breath and then, into the face of all the bullying father-figures of my life, I said, 'No.' Everyone else, I was later told, froze and expected the sky to come down.

But nothing happened. It was as if this tiny word, this splinter of honesty, had pricked a huge balloon filled with hot air. I heard a few mumbled words, and then the director came on stage and said calmly, almost sympathetically: 'All right, we'll do without the sound effects then.' The rehearsal went on, reasonably, and reasonably well, too.

Whether that was some sort of victory, and if so, whose it was, and over whom or what, I never worked out. In my remaining time there, our relationship was more relaxed, with a whiff, just a whiff, of irony and respect from both sides, I think I can say. Oh — and the actor who played Hamlet's father and who now supplied the ghostly commands himself, hidden among the hedges — he, of course, did it properly, a haunting roar, with plenty of metaphysical vibrato.

It Was the Nightingale

Recently a pair of friends returned to Ireland from a sabbatical year which they had spent in Berlin, their first visit to that city. And how had they found my hometown, the resurrected German metropolis? Almost with one voice, their eyes shining, they answered: We heard our first nightingale! I could well understand them — you don't forget your first and maybe only nightingale of a lifetime, just as you don't forget your first and maybe only comet. So I willingly heard their story, and then had to tell them mine. I had heard my first nightingale not in Berlin where they are in fact fairly common, but only after I departed from that city to work as an actor in the town of Hannover.

It was a beautiful May night and I had taken a different way home after our performance, along a sizeable lake not far from the town centre, the Masch See. I was walking amidst the light of street-lamps and traffic noise, but on the opposite shore was parkland, a full moon had risen above the black trees, glistening on the waters of the lake. As I walked it gradually came to me that the night air was filled with song, the sparkling waves and the sound of jubilation that I heard seemed one and the same thing. The time was past midnight — so these, then, had to be nightingales! When I stood still, there was just one, undivided, breathless chorus, but when I walked on, I could make out individual singers, one passing me on to the next. At the city end of the lake I focused on one particular bird, crossed a wide lawn and cautiously approached the bush on the riverbank from where he was singing. Eventually, nervous with excitement, I stood only a foot away from the dense foliage that hid that throbbing throat. For that is the most striking thing at such proximity: the unrestrained energy with which the song bursts forth. Unlike other birds, the nightingale combines a dazzling array of different tunes in his singing: liquid, beckoning notes are followed by sustained, searing calls of longing or a trumpeting, passionate crescendo. In between, deep silences and, imbedded into these, the sweetest, most moving tunes of all, only audible from such nearness: a sub-song, like a little, reflective soliloquy or a few tender words to his sitting mate — making you almost ashamed of listening in.

There I stood, in communion with all those who had ever stood so before — transfixed and enraptured by the song of songs. I felt as if I had been permitted, at last, into the inner sanctum of nature, the heart of the mystery beating only an arm's length away, but forever protected by a feeling of awe.

You don't keep an experience like that to yourself. So the next night I took a companion along, a young singer who appeared as an extra in our play, the only person I knew then who might sympathise with my sensations. We went to the same spot, the bird was there, and we had just settled into our listening when we were flushed, so to speak — a man, pulled along by an eager Alsatian, was approaching us. Our initial fright eased when we saw he was wearing a uniform, a policeman on patrol. He didn't seem at all surprised to find a man with a woman here in the darkness of the park and curtly asked for identification. What were we doing here? Listening to the nightingale, we hushed him, pointing to the bush where the bird had fallen silent. That reply rendered him speechless; he gave us a long glance and then made his dog sit. Silence returned, and the bird intoned again. Each one of us a step apart from the other, we stood and listened, an actor, a singer, a policeman, a dog. Below the singing we could hear the murmur of the river. A cool drizzle was descending upon us. The bird sang.

I don't know what the others felt, I only know that for me it was not like the night before. Perhaps because I was now the nightingale's promoter, or because one is never the same person at the same place twice — but there grew a distance in me this time, a cold realisation that this singing had nothing to do with me, or with mankind, no more, indeed, than the rain and the river, or the hidden moon and the stars above. The German poet Rainer Maria Rilke said that beauty was only the beginning of terror — perhaps I had an inkling of that, in those moments when the nightingale suddenly turned into clockwork. But then the policeman remembered his duties and gently told us that this was not really a prudent place at night, for a man and a woman, then saluted, and left. We stayed on for a few more minutes, but the spell was broken, and so we too made our way back across the wet grass. Behind us, the song of our very own nightingale melted back into the jubilant chorus. For them, nothing had changed.

Per Aspera Etc.

With every little movement he makes, his bed gnashes its teeth, its frame propped up on wobbly bricks, their surfaces grinding against each other. The room he is in is a caricature of wretchedness, but he can't laugh. Apart from the bed it contains a chair, a tiny table and some hooks on the walls. The slip of space that leads to the door is so narrow he has to move sideways. This former pantry of a once splendid apartment is all he can afford at the moment, as an unemployed actor in West Berlin. He has returned here, after a two-year stint at a theatre in West Germany which had led nowhere, artistically. In Berlin he had hoped to pick up some strands he had left lying here. But there were no welcomes, no prospects, only guarded promises and vague hopes for a distant future. At the labour exchange they had told him, with a thin smile, that there were 2,000 unemployed actors in Berlin. So now he is No. 2001. His teachers in the drama school who had high hopes for him are barely able to conceal their disappointment and impatience; his mother gives him her long, worried glances; his stepfather treats him to a sarcastic silence — he is not surprised.

The bed is gnashing its teeth. He's tossing and turning, sleeplessness is setting its teeth into his life. It's true that this situation has always been on the cards. What had he expected? Certainly not an instant, shining career. Somehow he had expected to be allowed to serve, as his cultural background and his acting teachers had taught him to do, to serve the author, the production, the cast, and for himself he would add, the language, the language in which he is discovering his own humanity. To serve — but, as it appears now, on his own terms. Is this the problem — his pride? Or is he, indeed, the 'anti-actor', as he had been called by the director in his last job? In the cruel hours of early morning, on a gnashing bed-frame, nervously, sexually exhausted, he can see himself having been wrong from the start, dumped already as useless, as surplus, as waste, in this tiny, damp box of a cell, before being ground down, slowly, as so many were before him, by the maws of the metropolis. Even if he now decided, in the throes of his desperation and self-pity, to jump from the fourth floor into the courtyard below, he would fail, for the miserable slit of a window would not let him through.

One day a telegram arrives: a small theatre on the edge of Germany, by the North Sea coast, needs the Lorenzo for a production of *The Merchant of Venice* — would he be interested?

Next morning he is on the train. With every minute, every mile passing, he feels more liberated, more confident of having a future after all. Beyond Hamburg the landscape becomes ever flatter, until all that's left is a boundless, green plain and a huge sky, all bathed in an immense lucidity, even now, in late autumn. He sees, for the first time, the wind-shorn trees, all hurrying, strangely enough, in the direction he is fleeing from. Then, towards the end of his journey, beacons, lighthouses, enigmatic signs with numbers and letters, peeping over the dike that's running parallel with the railway-track — symbols of orientation, of a focused, purposeful landscape. He feels he can't get lost here, in this small, sober town, comfortable behind its protective system of canals, sluice-gates and dams. He falls for the place, instantly.

The audition goes smoothly. He has a prompt rapport with the director. He has studied the part, and he gets it. After the first night, his contract is extended for the entire year. After a few more productions, people start talking about having a star in their little town. But that is later. For the moment, night after night, he revels in speaking some of the most beautiful lines in all of classical drama, Lorenzo's words about love, and music and the harmony of the celestial spheres: 'The moon shines bright: in such a night as this, when the sweet wind did gently kiss the trees and they did make no noise …'

On such a night as this, he becomes aware of a brightness in one of the front rows, a face shining like a hazy moon in the near-darkness of the auditorium. In the interval, through the peep-hole in the curtain, he sees her more clearly. And again, a few days later, in the town library, where she works as a trainee. In daylight her face is sunshine. He speaks to her, invites her to the next show, a love story, where he plays the lead. She accepts. After the performance he walks her home, along the shore, through a glittering winter night.

Soon afterwards they become lovers. There is no hesitation. They've met at the right moment. Their relationship is public enough, the true extent of it, though, has to be shrouded in exquisite secrecy. For a while, fickle Fate holds them in the palm of her hand, caringly. They love, they work, they learn. Their cup is very full.

His heart is flooded with gratitude; he feels an urge to find some gesture, some small, sacrificial act to give expression to his thankfulness. One Saturday morning he takes her to the local petshop. There is a cage with a number of captured wild birds. He points at a goldfinch. The owner's hand of Fate grabs the panicking little thing and stuffs him into a small cardboard box. After paying, they go to the town park. There, on the ramparts of the old castle, he opens the box and holds it up into the air. It takes the bird a moment to catch up with this latest twist of Fate, but then, like an arrow, with a short, liquid call, it shoots out into freedom, a little, dark fleck that soon dissolves into the blinding spring light. Left behind, they kiss.

Not a Fairy Tale

Once upon a time I was an evil dwarf. *The* Evil Dwarf, to be more precise. Of course, I only acted the part, but even so, to be good at it, you had to unearth everything in yourself that was bad and dwarfish and drag it up into the limelight. I was then working as an actor at a small city-theatre in North Germany. That year's Christmas pantomime was *Snow White and Rose Red*, one of the Grimm fairytales, grim indeed because of this Evil Dwarf, hoarder of a large treasure, deep in the forest, after stealing it from the beautiful prince and turning him into an ugly bear. But, of course, he gets his comeuppance in the end!

I must have been a convincing blackguard, for night after night the children hated me, heckling continuously and screaming with delight at the dwarf's climactic trouncing by the big bear. I was helped by a most inspired costume: dark, spindly legs, a big hump covered by a coat made of withered leaves, a long, thinnish beard, like cobwebs, and coal-black eyes under a pale thatch of dried grass out of which grew a wickedly crooked red root — a twilight creature, rising out of the forest floor and melting back into it. But like every good ham worth his salt, I also saw him as a tragically misunderstood being — to no avail, I have to admit, as the children wanted their villain pure and simple. Except on one occasion.

We had travelled deep into the cultural wasteland of the North German plain to perform in a huge community hall, as stimulating and inviting as an airport hangar. Over a thousand children had been bussed to the place, for the great cultural event of the season if not of all their childhood years. And they were a wonderfully attentive and lively audience — for whom all the characters of the play, Bear, Woodcutter, the Girls and the Evil Dwarf, wove their magic spell. My most provocative moment came: having done my evil worst, I jumped up and down with glee — rubbing my black-nailed claws, my hump bumping, the withered red root on my head twitching — and proclaimed triumphantly: TO BE EVIL IS FUN! Noooo! A thousand voices screamed back at me. Oh yes, it is! Nooooo! A thousand voices screamed back again. Oh yes, it is! And: Noooo! again. For me it was like standing in the full blast of a hundred jet-engines, the air thick with disapproval. The Evil Dwarf, of course, was in his element; wallowing in it, he worked the crowd of little innocents for what it was worth. And then the totally unexpected, the absolutely unexpectable happened.

In the middle of all the turmoil, the jumping and screaming, a tiny little girl in the front row stood up — a blonde, blue-eyed snowflake — and shyly, yet like somebody who deep inside knew exactly what she was doing, walked up to the ramp, so terribly close to the dreadful dwarf, raised her arm — and offered me a sweet! To a howl of protest from a thousand other kids. And went back to her seat.

How to react to that? I was speechless, totally deflated. But also, as an actor, I felt deeply understood and appreciated. The frozen heart had to melt for a moment; I thanked her awkwardly, took the sweet and ate it. And then had to work

hard for the rest of the evening to regain my evil reputation —
the show had to go on.

Since then, I have often wondered what had gone on in the
mind of that little girl and what became of her in later years —
a child who at the age of four or five had risked her life to
bring solace to another being who was ugly and unhappy, and
evil.

A Vandal Scandal

It was a successful midsummer night's party, and when the sun rose we were all deliriously, boisterously drunk. *We* were the actors, mostly young, of a small theatre in a small North German town on the North Sea coast, and the party had been given by one of our stalwart supporters, a young local woman with a tolerant husband and a big house, who adored the arts, and the theatre especially, and one or two of the actors in particular. It was hot in the house, somebody suggested an early morning swim. We ran down to the beach and stripped, intent on throwing ourselves into the foaming brine. But there was no brine — the tide was out, and when the tide is out on these shores, it is out for miles. All we could manage was to splash each other with water that barely reached our ankles and catch glimpses of our unenticing bare essentials, a healthy antidote to the smouldering passions it was our job to enact on stage. These letdowns should have sobered us up a bit, but they didn't.

Back on the beach, we discovered sandcastles, a whole colony of them. Now it may not be generally known, but it is scientifically proven that the German race possesses an extra gene in their chromosomal make-up, making them different from all other peoples. This extra gene forces them, forces them — to start building sandcastles the moment their toes touch sand. It's involuntary, they can't do anything about it, it's an instinct. And here now they had created a whole city of ring-forts, each one surrounding its own wickerwork beach chair, that peculiarly German invention for people who want to sizzle in the sun on cold, windy beaches. The castles were ingeniously designed and finished, elaborately decorated with little flags and mussel-shells and separated by orderly pathways. Beautiful!

But on this early Sunday morning we discovered there may yet be another extra gene present in the German people, but only in a small minority group, namely young actors, a gene that is only activated by the intake of copious amounts of alcohol. A gene that forces young actors to raze sandcastles to the ground as they come upon them — they can't help it, it's a natural drive. And this we did, like Vikings, with relish, and thoroughly. 'Down with the values of the bourgeoisie!' we shouted — we, whose existence depended on these very same values! 'Down with the shameful appropriation of public space by private greed!' — or words to that effect. Or maybe no coherent words at all, just wild and increasingly breathless laughter as our trampling legs did their worst on works of popular art.

Having thus accomplished our biological mission, we turned our attention to the still sleeping little town for some further rearrangements. Out of a most tidily kept front garden we lifted a heavy wrought-iron bench and placed it on the pavement outside — turned, so that the general public could rest there and admire this exemplary front garden. In a quiet one-way street we hoisted a few of the more lightly built cars and reversed their direction, leaving their owners to wonder the following day whether they had driven backwards into the road. Then we presented the ladies among us with generous bunches of flowers, borrowed from private and public gardens — after which my memory withdraws from the scene, as we ourselves must have done.

To the rehearsal on Monday morning one of us brought a copy of the local paper. There, on the front page, was an article headlined: 'VANDALS IN DUHNEN!' The story reported how the previous night vandals had destroyed a large number of sandcastles on Duhnen beach which had been lovingly built by their owners (there it was: owners!) for the big Sandcastle Competition on Sunday afternoon, forcing a postponement. The shock made us blush and grow pale in quick succession. The town's pride and joy, the theatre, was harbouring — vandals! What if it came out? A scandal! The repercussions could well be serious for us, for the survival of the theatre was dependent on the good-will of the city fathers, and the good burghers' faithful turnout at our performances. Our frolicking rebelliousness of two mornings before shrivelled into — plain vandalism. For a few days the threat of being unmasked hung over our heads. We kept our mouths shut though, and soon the whole thing was forgotten. But that was the worst review I ever got in this town, Hamlet the Vandal! What's worse, I have to admit, to this day I'm not entirely unproud of it.

A Riding Lesson

Thanks to Flann O'Brien's famous 'Mollycule Theory', we are now in a position to understand why horsy people give birth to four-legged ideas, and why the minds of cyclists go round in circles; atomic exchange is the explanation, unavoidable in the course of protracted rumbustious contact. I myself am becoming increasingly aware of the presence of ferric oxide (rust) in my system, due, no doubt, to my many years on the back of a bike. But no detector will ever find even a single horse-molecule in my physical or mental make-up. Here is the reason why not.

As a young actor I once spent a couple of weeks doing open-air theatre on a huge stage that had been cut out of the bog in East Friesland. East Friesland, which borders the Netherlands, used to be all bog, and it is the home of the German equivalent of the Kerryman jokes, although it has to be admitted that our East Friesland variety never reaches the subtlety and sheer elegance of the Irish versions. They are more — earthbound, if you like. For instance: What are the deep ditches for, on both sides of the roads in Friesland? — So that the Frieslanders, when walking about, can swing their arms! Or why have the Frieslanders such rounded backs? — Because the burghers of Bremen used to ride to work on them! — That kind of — eh, humour.

First Station

East Friesland is also as flat as its other neighbour, the North Sea, which was unfortunate, artistically speaking, seeing our afternoon play for children was a cowboy-and-Indian drama set in the Rocky Mountains, while our evening play *Wilhelm Tell* took place in the Swiss Alps. So my story has to be imagined as happening in front of a timid heap of cardboard rocks, piled up by our stage designer in a losing battle against the horizontal immensity of the East Friesian sky.

Redskins ride mustangs. The Count Rudenz I played in *Tell* was to prance onto the stage on a magnificent steed. That was the idea. But the only horses we were able to hire in this deeply agricultural area were giant Trakehners, those heavy-booted, wide-backed work-horses we sometimes see in beer ads on TV. And, as working horses, they were not available to us working actors until the very last moment, namely our dress rehearsal. Which was public. But we had been assured there would be no problems, the horses being absolutely good-natured and docile.

The afternoon performance came. I, Chief Little Wolf, was to ride bareback, of course, for authenticity. Yet when I managed to get on top of my mountain of flesh, my legs stuck out on both sides like oars from a curragh. There was no way of exerting any pressure on those bulging flanks under me. My cue came. My horse stood. And wouldn't budge. In panic, somebody gave him a slap and he condescended to stir. My directions had been to gallop centre-stage, stop, rearing up, if possible, yell a warning to the assembled tribe and gallop off again. Instead, we now moved across the whole width of the stage without stopping in a sleepy trot, with me popping up and down on the horse's flat back like a ping-pong ball, until we disappeared on the other side into the greenery. That was pretty bad.

In *Wilhelm Tell* we had originally envisioned me riding swiftly on stage, grandly dismounting and then proceeding to have a poignant encounter with my beloved. Forewarned by the afternoon's disaster, my horse and I were now led — plod, plod, plod — by a stableman. When we had arrived centre-stage he commanded: Brrr! And my fiery charger wobbled to a halt. I now attempted to jump off, musketeer-style, flying cape and all. But one leg got caught in the cape and the other stuck in the stirrup; ensnared by the reins, wrapped in my cloak like a bat in hibernation, I slowly sank, head first, down the horse's flank. Stableman and noble lady between them had to pluck me from my entanglement. Whereupon my glorious self had to stride, with my beloved, to the ramp and ask for her hand in marriage. The audience groaned.

It was there and then, from the depth of my misery, that my whole being, body and soul, took a vow: Never, never, never again!

And I never broke it. Not even many years later, already here in Ireland, when a lady friend invited me along on one of her outings on horseback. While I walked in the bright April sunshine, she passed me by on her mount — joyfully erect, her eyes gleaming with the bliss of both control and abandon, her lovely breasts nodding at me encouragingly — the goddess Diana, a vision of harmony between animal and woman. Later she suggested a riding lesson on her horse, who was all calmness and docility, she said. Oh no, I'd heard that one before! I didn't even touch the beast!

Swimming in the Dark

One sultry summer night, many years ago, a young woman and a young man who found it difficult to be with each other and impossible to be without, rode their bikes down to the bay. It was around midnight and the beach was deserted. Silently the woman undressed and stepped into the tepid water, striding forward purposefully until it was deep enough to swim. The man followed. They had not talked about this. There was no choice. The water was phosphorescent, each wavelet, each movement of their hands stirred up a shower of twinkling sparks. They swam, makers of light. As the woman moved ahead with calm, even strokes, he saw her head trailing a luminous wake, instead of the shining blonde hair of day. That he followed.

The bay opened out into the estuary of a very big river. The woman swam straight ahead towards the open sea. Did she know what she was doing? Did she care? Was this an act of despair, or one of abandonment, of communion with the elements, with water and night? He had no idea, but he followed her, making his own observations.

There was an electric storm raging above the land on the other side of the river. Lightning shone in great convulsions, but in total silence, because of the distance. And on their own side another storm was building up, with blinding discharges, but again there was as yet no thunder. They were swimming between two dark curtains torn by erupting flashes, while directly above them the sky was clear and flooded with stars. And their every movement caused an outbreak of countless tiny lights that mirrored the immense splendour overhead. Wordlessly they swam, the woman leading, the man following doggedly. They were by now far out; soon one would have to be reasonable and think about turning back.

Slowly a fear began to spread in his mind and body. Was she suicidal, had she lost her senses? Was she fleeing from him, or was she luring him on? Was this a test, a trial, a challenge? To him, to herself, to them both? For a mad, self-forgotten moment he thought that he didn't care, that he would follow her until death should take them both — but at that moment something firm and smooth touched him, a body slowly gliding alongside his own. His first idea in this uncanny setting was that he had bumped into a corpse; he was clutched by panic. But then there came another one, and another, and he realised they must be jellyfish. But the first shock lingered on; they were not alone anymore in the wide, benevolent sea, there were other, sinister presences lurking. He tried to sound calm and rational: 'I think it's enough now!' She did not react. Maybe she did not listen. She swam on. After some frighteningly endless minutes, she suddenly stopped, turned around, passed him without speaking or looking, and headed back. This time they swam side by side, albeit at a distance, and stepped out of the water, together.

And stayed together for a good many years, for many good years. But they never talked to each other about their nocturnal swim. And you could say that all through those years they never truly left that light-encircled, haunted bay.

Part III

Here and There

Of Mushrooms and Men

Hallimasch, Reizker and Bovist, Egerling, Steinpilz, Morchel and Ziegenbart, Grünling, Bläuling, Rötling — autumn is the time to go out and look for them, wild mushrooms, those strangely shaped, beautifully coloured beings springing up overnight here and there and everywhere, but in particular profusion in the dappled light of the forest floor. The words above are German, just a few of many colourful, descriptive, but most of all magically evoking, names. My English guide-book, in contrast, comes up with only a handful of English names, the enormous difference in numbers perhaps indicating the much greater role the forest and its denizens play in the German and, indeed, Continental landscape and culture, both high and popular.

Looking for mushrooms invokes the hunting-and-gathering instincts in us; they hide, they vary their locations and times of appearance; normally you have to do a lot of walking and stalking before you can hunt them down and gather them in. Although occasionally it works the other way round, and they find you. The mushroom picker carries an inner map of the forest around with him or her, an emotionally charged one. I, for instance, shall never forget and always return to the spot in the Wicklow Mountains where I was once — so far only once! — treated to an abundance of ceps, the most sought-after of all the fungi, or the place which, on one memorable outing, I found plastered with tightly packed chanterelles. You feel inexplicably but justly rewarded on such days, as if you were only given your due. And on another memorable occasion, many years ago, I think I witnessed how the finding of an unusual mushroom had an even deeper and more lasting effect on a fellow human being.

In 1970 I was doing a spell of work experience in a home for juvenile offenders. The place was tucked away deep in the forests of the Eifel, a mountain range south-west of Cologne. The boys under my care were 13- to 15-year olds. Taken away from their usual stomping grounds and troubled families in the big cities of the Ruhr Valley, they were just normal, lovely lads, if maybe a bit more in need of attention and direction, not to mention human warmth, than others. There were a few interesting characters among them, but Dieter was not one of them; in fact Dieter was actually the opposite of a character, and not in any apparent way interesting. He was lowest in the group's pecking order and, it has to be said, understandably so. Lacking all physical or intellectual graces, heavily built and heavily witted, he gave the impression of being completely resigned to his shortcomings, of even revelling in them. Forever ingratiating himself with the others through self-belittlement, all he got for it of course was contempt. I, too, found having Dieter around a grating experience and I needed to focus fully on my educational mission to be fair to him.

The Catholic sisters who ran the home were reluctant to bring the boys out into the forest, but I was given free range to do so, and it was on one of these roamings that an excited cry suddenly rang out for me to come quickly, Dieter had found something! And that something was really some thing! A huge, beige-grey ball lay there in the leaf-mould, the size of a pumpkin; no, not a giant puff-ball, as I thought for a moment, more like a giant cauliflower or a huge globe of crumpled paper. Dieter knelt beside it, his arms around it, guarding it like his baby. None of us had ever seen such a weird mushroom before. In procession we brought it back to the home, with Dieter in front, carrying the thing in his arms, his chin and a beaming grin resting on top of it. Nobody in the home had any idea what Dieter's monster could be, so we called on the highest local authority in such matters, the forester. He came, added his amazement to ours, but had no name for the object either. After consulting his books at home, he rang back later in the evening, saying it was Sparassis Laminosa — also known as Echter Ziegenbart, or Bärentatze, or Blumenkohlpilz, or Krause Glucke. That is, Goat's Beard, Bear's Paw, Cauliflower Fungus or Sitting Hen — names that may give an idea of the thing's fantastic appearance. It was not only exceedingly rare but also deemed excellent for human consumption, and so it was sacrificed, and our whole group, some 15 people, had an opulent meal of Cauliflower Fungus that night.

Dieter, from that day on, was no longer the Dieter we had grown to know and dislike. There was a new confidence and purpose in his demeanour, a new-found pride in himself. Instead of seeing the thing and kicking it, as a surrogate football, into smithereens, he had recognised it for what it was, something extraordinary, something unique, and in that recognition he had found himself. For the first time in his life he had been one of the chosen few on whom Nature had visibly bestowed one of her more precious gifts. The other boys, too, the nuns and myself, all of us now saw him in a different light, and gave him praise and a measure of respect. And that I think, or hope, helped Dieter towards a greater sense of his own worth, and towards a healing of the wounds he and all of these kids had already suffered and were carrying forward into their adult years.

There is a little addendum to this story: last autumn, in the Wicklow Mountains, I stumbled across a virtual twin of Dieter's monster, and the events of 30 years ago came back to me. I, too, felt irrationally proud of myself, as if Gaia, the Earth Goddess, had singled me out and smiled at me. You can always do with such an experience. The book says the fungus is prone to reappear year after year at the same spot. So there may be hope for this most pleasant encounter to repeat itself, perhaps even annually. But should I really wish for that? I'm not so sure.

Assorted Gifts

When we visited a very, very remote part of Ireland for a few summer days in the early Seventies, several people told us that Christmas was the best time to come here, that Christmas here was the real thing! Imagining that holiday in Ireland to be basically the same as at home in Germany — silent, homely, adorned with traditional customs — we decided to spend our first Irish Christmas there on the Atlantic seaboard, at one of the many ends of the world.

There had been a slight hesitation in the voice of MJ, the hotel-owner, before he accepted our telephone booking, and when we arrived we saw a young woman we recognised from our summer visit as his girlfriend, hastily leave the house in what looked suspiciously like a last-minute escape. It turned out we were the only guests in an unheated hotel. Our room was tastefully painted in pastel colours, if austerely furnished. We started to stow away our few things and, opening a little cupboard beside the wash-basin, found something that literally took our breath away: there stood a chamberpot, filled to the rim with what it was designed for — a highly personal welcome from the previous occupants of our room, a considerable time ago, judging from its appearance. Angrily amused, we got rid of the stuff in the toilet next door and, as the room was freezing, slipped straight away between the nylon sheets for a bit of warmth and rest after an arduous journey by train and bus and, finally, on foot. Whatever the circumstances, for the moment we were marooned.

We awoke in darkness. This was Christmas Eve, the very hub of events for German children which we, despite being two 30-somethings, still at heart were, especially on this night. The hotel was dead quiet, so we set out to find the famous Christmas of these parts. We tried the pub. Now we had seen crowded pubs before, but this was of a different order. The hovel was crammed, stuffed to the gills with humanity, mainly men, all in a state of advanced drunkenness. We were sucked in as to a whirlpool, then squeezed forward between slowly swaying bodies. The lights were few and dim, the smoke as dense as the noise. Welcomes were shouted at us from mouths in amazing states of dental disrepair. I felt transported back in time into the paintings of Brueghel or Bosch. If this smouldering, smoking airlessness was not Hell, it was surely Purgatory, the meeting place of desperately merry, lonely souls. One such soul, a hairy-nosed individual, was mysteriously insistent in his approaches, whispering into my ear that he knew, nudge, nudge, that he could tell me things, wink, wink — what could he be hinting at? Other voices told him to shut up. When we had been treated to more whiskeys than we could hold in two hands, we quietly panicked and managed to slip out of the back door, leaving the bar-room behind like a tightly packed firecracker about to explode.

Out in the open, all was expanse — the bogland, the beach, the sea. The starry sky. A frosty night. We walked through the scattered village. Here and there sparks shot out of chimneys and faded among the Milky Way. Then, calls leapt to and fro between two houses, in a language we did not understand — our first words of living Irish, making us feel foreign and welcome at the same time. Then again glittering silence — a silent night, if not a holy one.

Late next morning as I traipsed through the quiet hotel, I heard a feeble voice calling for me. I found the mighty MJ in his bedroom, a small, dark cubicle, unfurnished, with layers of newspaper instead of a carpet. MJ lay on a mattress on the floor, crooked with pain, covered with just one flimsy blanket. It's the kidneys, he moaned. I was shocked and offered to get help, maybe ring the doctor? Oh, no no no, just a cup of tea, that would be nice! Deeply worried, I proceeded to make that cup of tea and brought it to him, my Christmas gift, humble indeed, a cup of tea, presented to the host by the guest. He was touchingly grateful and told me that if we wanted breakfast or, indeed, a Christmas dinner, we would unfortunately have to cook it ourselves, but we would find the turkey in the fridge!

After breakfast we took a walk through the dunes and along the beach. It was a bright, icy day; the sun was blinding and threw our long, black shadows onto a landscape of stark, unremitting contrasts. For quite a while we lingered at a place where a number of curraghs had been pulled up high on the shore and turned upside-down for wintering. The sunlight was reflected in long, bright stripes on their black skins, giving them a tragic air, like a shoal of beached whales, but at the same time they were the only sign of human activity, for we didn't meet a single human soul on that afternoon stroll down the long shore. Only when we had returned to the road and were heading back towards the village, did we see two figures coming our way. Our initial relief gradually turned into disquiet, however, when we couldn't make out whether they were young or old, male or female, or, the thought momentarily struck us, even human. They came in our direction with strange, jerky, then again dance-like movements, wearing oversized, dark, shapeless garments, nor could we make sense of their oddly coloured and misshapen heads. It was only when they were a hundred yards away from us that we realised they were wearing masks. One was like a mask from a classical Greek play, wide-open, with frenzied eye-sockets and a twisted mouth; the other, if anything, was even more frightening for being almost featureless, like a white balaclava with a few dark smudges on it. Closing in, they moved around us in a half-circle, watching our timidly smiling faces, as we looked into the black eye-holes of their masks. We heard a few subdued laughs or grunts, and then the distance between them and us grew again as we headed in opposite directions. Both they and we kept turning around but we couldn't make up our minds whether their waving arms looked like greetings or threats. We were by now fairly disoriented.

Later in the evening, while my wife was struggling with the bulk of the bird and the remarkable condition of the kitchen, I was taken aside by one of the previous night's revellers who today had reassembled in the hotel bar. With rituals of utter secrecy he enlightened me about last night's strange intimations in the pub, the locals having formed the opinion that I was the German paymaster of the IRA — why else would a German come to this God-forsaken place at this ungodly time of the year — though he expressed himself somewhat more colloquially. My appalled face must have put paid to their theory, for the issue was not followed up any further. But at least our visit had presented them with food for talk and fantasising.

Our Christmas dinner for two was an even greater success: next morning we found the turkey reduced to a mere skeleton. The hungry lions and hyenas we had heard roaring and laughing all through the night in the bar downstairs had sniffed out a Christmas gift to them and subsequently picked it clean. Time for ourselves to think about our own disappearance. We were lucky: a minibus had been organised for the young people who had come home from abroad; they would simply move a bit closer and give us a lift to the town where we would get our train. At every farm gate there were embraces and floods of tears, and then in the bus sobs and silences. But gradually youth and neighbourliness won out, as talk and laughter returned. We looked around into tired, tear-stained, smiling faces, and as our vehicle criss-crossed the countryside, its windows fogging over from all the life it held within, and as biscuits and sweets were handed round, and everybody was generously included in the sharing of everything — then, at last, the two foreigners felt that they had arrived at their Irish Christmas, now, at the very moment they were leaving it.

Couples

We were a few years into our marriage when we spent a fortnight's holiday in a very remote part of Ireland. The remoteness had been the reason for our choice of the place: we had a need, as young couples sometimes do, to confront the vast empty spaces of sea and sky and bogland with our closeness, with the miracle of it. That things turned out differently was probably not caused by the gloomy atmosphere in the hotel, nor by the depressing weather, but by an inner necessity we had been carrying with us. It was during those days that we had the first inkling of a gap at the very core of our togetherness, an unbridgeable cleft which, like a germinating seed, could only grow with time. We still had many years of married life before us, and nothing dramatic happened then, no rows, no tears; in the nights we still tried to hold on passionately, that is desperately, to what cannot be held. But when we looked out into the surrounding nebulous landscape veiled in rain, we were looking into ourselves, and the incongruous shape of the double-decker bus which floated twice a day through the mist and dusk, like a darkly threatening vision, each time heightened our discomfort. It always arrived empty there at the terminus, and always left empty too. During those two weeks, nobody came to the hotel, and only two people departed.

They were the only other guests, a couple like ourselves, but middle-aged. All we ever saw of them was the wife coming from their room and hurrying back to it, a pale, dark-haired woman dressed in black, like a widow. She was looking after her husband who, we were told, was ill and unable to leave his bed. Meals were brought to their room, once I saw the tray as it was collected — the food had hardly been touched.

One late afternoon there was a slight commotion in the hotel, a taxi had arrived for the departure of the two. The driver went up to them to give the lady a hand. When they came down, the husband, his arms over their shoulders, dangled between them like an emaciated puppet, his feet barely touching the ground. The colour of his shining, childish face was a high orange-red: a broad, silly grin and hands waving limply right and left gave a jolly farewell to anyone around. The woman's head was bent in shame, the taxi-man's face professionally blank. And then they were gone. When we later passed the open door of their room, the landlady called us in. 'Look at that!' she said in shock. The space under the bed was crammed with empty whiskey bottles.

Now we were alone with our hosts, a youngish couple who had only recently bought the house and were in the process of renovating it. There was something half-hearted, though, about the man's activity, unfinished jobs lurked everywhere, and his wife's attempts at hospitality were hardly more convincing. Both were working away wordlessly, doggedly, but without any coordination. With our newly opened eyes we seemed to see how only this huge undertaking of restoring and running a run-down hotel was holding them together, and that without it they would both be far away, and far apart.

Then it was our turn to leave. We were sitting in the lounge, waiting for the bus. As there was some time to fill, I was scribbling in my diary, trying to capture what was slipping by; my wife was browsing in a couple of old guest-books she had found on a rubble-skip. Suddenly she stood before me, her face agleam with the joy of discovery. 'Look what I've found!' she said and placed the book on my knees.

There I saw entries from ten years before, June 1964. Five people had signed the page, all with Liverpool addresses: Water St, Castle St, Dale St, Bold St. Neat entries, including the 'Remarks' column. A woman had confided in the guest-book: 'Great to have John on his own, and no fans!' And husband John had added: 'Cynthia and I had a swinging time!' A fellow called Paul had uttered a sigh of relief: 'A great weekend, and with no fans in sight!' A man named George was more laconic: 'I love it, yeah, yeah, yeah!' And finally: 'Nice to let your hair down!' That came from a guest who had signed, Ringo.

Names and words like guitar-chords, ringing out in a major key. The place lit up, and so did our spirits. People had been happy here, a whole weekend long. And wasn't it possible that even love-songs had had their secret origin here, in the Crossroads Hotel?

An Instrument Sublime

One is hardly ever present when poems are being born, except, of course, if one is the poet, and even then he or she may have doubts about their total presence of mind. In any case, should you witness the arrival of a poem, the event may well turn out to be as amazing, even unnerving, and certainly as unforgettable, as a birth in the flesh.

The story of Davoren Hanna is widely known — his affliction from birth with various, most debilitating physical handicaps, his and his parents' overcoming of the wall of silence between them with the help of typed-out messages, his short but brilliant career as a poet, his early death in 1994.

We happened to know his parents from before the births of Davoren and Aengus, our own son, born in the same year, and it is one of the great blessings of my life that we kept in touch and were able to follow the Davoren Hanna story at some proximity. As a memorial to one of their visits to our house, I still possess a pitiable little scrap of paper which contains an astonishing piece of poetry.

After the traditional late arrival of the three, after welcomes and apologies, after all the nervous little ceremonies of people visiting in each other's territories, after the torturous feeding of Davoren, torturous for himself and for those who had to do or watch it — after all that, things finally settled down and Dav was ready for communication. Out came the old portable typewriter, a piece of paper was put in, and soon we could read Dav's greeting to his hosts, typically in the form of praise: 'Your family satisfaction is apparent!' We blushed. Then followed a discussion about a play they had seen in the theatre, and he was asked his opinion. 'The lighter aspects of the sequences were a howl, but the serious moments were boring' — a well-rounded indictment from a 13-year-old. Next, on the scrap of paper, some word-splinters, hinting at what was to follow. Just two words: 'Sexy of.' Then a question to the woman of the house: 'Was Aengus your favourite little scallywag?' And an order to his own mother, Brighid: 'Send my knicker poem to Aengus!' The few lines that now followed made it abundantly clear what was occupying his mind at this moment:

Great Sexpectations

The boys say diddies
The girls say willies
Why do children giggle
And why do bottoms wiggle?

Everyone burst out laughing; there were a few half-serious motherly protests, but Dav beamed with glee, having stirred up this cosy middle-class, middle-aged suburban Sunday afternoon. Suddenly, in the middle of all the banter, he indicated he would now say something serious. Everyone watched and waited in anticipation. Then, after the usual mental and physical struggle that exhausted them both, Brighid read it out for us in her most matter-of-fact voice:

Denial

Was Daniel always lonely

While in his lions' den?
Was he jealous of the daylight
Astride the horizon?

Shadows play solo music
On an instrument sublime.

We shook our heads in confusion. Where did this come
from, literally minutes after 'Great Sexpectations'? What did
it mean? Brighid was able to give some tentative
interpretations: Dav had recently been deeply affected by the
biblical story of Daniel (oh yes, there was this word-play
between 'denial' and 'Daniel'!), by that man's lonely
exposure to the brute forces of nature; moreover he had by
now, and most painfully, realised that his degree of handicap
would probably exclude him forever from a joyful sexual
partnership, accepting also that poetry was to be his only
chance of liberation and communion. That was really what the
poem was about, wasn't it? But that didn't explain its poetic
glories: those two searing questions, the breathtaking image of
the daylight making love to the horizon, the humble majesty of
the last two lines!

It's only now, after a good number of years, that I have
come to a fuller understanding of what happens in this poem.
A 13-year-old boy takes on his double cross of unfulfilment
and the gift of poetry, and accepts what it takes many of us a
lifetime to come to terms with: that we are instruments, maybe
sublime ones.

Going to the Dogs

Would I ever go to a dog-show? Hardly — so the dog-show had to come to me. One beautiful Saturday morning last summer there was an unusual accumulation of sound building up on an open space beyond our garden wall: a staccato of car doors banging, human greetings and commands, and a chorus of dog voices echoing from all directions. My curiosity raised, I decided to go — between the shopping and the lawn-mowing — and have a look.

Yes, a dog-show was getting into full swing, a national event, with participants from all over the country, north and south. Both the human and the canine species are innately gregarious — everywhere there were joyful encounters and reunions, within each species and across the divide — wagging tails and wagging tongues and shining faces all around! Everybody was having a party, and a highly organised one, too, all centred around the judging rings where the dog-and-owner pairs are circling the stern-faced judges like fairground carousels. But I, the first-time visitor, am more interested in collecting impressions.

Soon I'm wading knee-deep, thigh-high in a sea of dogs — strangely enough without feeling wary about my legs, for they are all as sweet and well-behaved as children at the beginning of a birthday party. For instance that huddle of five Shi Tzus, Tibetan lap-dogs, sitting prettily on their plastic table over

there. Their silky hair has been lovingly coifed, each dog
wears a pink bow on top of its head. As I walk past them they
follow my passage in a fascinated, synchronised movement,
like chorus girls stunned into awe and silence as the star of the
show passes by. I feel flattered: what do they see in me that
other beings don't?

Oh, look! — a bull-terrier, one of those dreaded killer
dogs, all muscles, powerful jaws and baleful, slanted eyes. He
is barked at, from within one of the collapsible, portable cages
which are everywhere, by a noble-nosed, elegantly limbed
borzoi, not aggressively, really more for camaraderie or sport.
With one great leap the terrible terrier jumps up at his pretty
young mistress, clutching her be-denimed thigh with all the
might of his front legs. And will not let go, his head turned
back in sheer terror at the other dog, the borzoi in the cage.
'Oh, you old cry-baby, you!' the girl chides her gormless
fighting machine.

Next to them reposes a massive mastiff, calm as a Buddha,
in deep contemplation of a few doggy biscuits in front of him
on a shiny plate. His multiple chins are covered by a bib
which he wears with the mien of a king.

And *there* is a heart-warming sight, a case of natural
justice: a huge St Bernard has decided to pay a visit to a
friend, and drags his helplessly stumbling, vainly protesting
owner along — the exact image, in reverse, of the one so
frequently seen, of a human pulling away a struggling little
dog.

That is the general impression; here, humans are at the
service of the dogs. Everywhere there is grooming going on,
combing, brushing and blow-drying, for extra fluffiness and
shine. Sprays and powders are brought into action, nails and

tails are being trimmed — all in the quest for the perfect image, the ideal presentation. Not to mention the underlying centuries of genetic engineering which have produced so many breeds, colours, sizes and tempers; there are warriors and labourers, clowns and aristocrats, boudoir creatures and all-weather types — a dog people, created in our own image, a subject race to serve our needs, our pleasures and whims, and our yen for competition. And they, in their infinite patience and dependence, they are going along with us. On a leash.

Even here, though, amidst all the hullabaloo of Vanity Fair, I see one or another of the dogs suddenly freeze into a statue of stone, all their senses focused on something far out, at the edge of their horizon. Where we can't detect a thing. Maybe they can't fully either, maybe they are only visited in such moments by a faint memory of a distant past. In any case, we can't follow them there. They have shaken us off.

189 Christmas Trees

It all must have started soon after my son's birth, when he was still in his pram, and his little face lit up when the branches of the tree under which he was parked in the front garden were swaying in the wind. We told him *Baum*!, the German for 'tree', and he loved the sound of the word, and laughed, and wanted to hear it again and again. It must have imprinted itself on his mind, a seed which sprouted and grew into an astonishing tree of knowledge. Soon we had to add more words on our walks with him: oak and birch and rowan and poplar and pine and sycamore and willow — all those beautiful, resounding, evocative names. And then my repertoire ran out and I had to resort to books on trees, and I read a lot and learned a lot through the unquenchable thirst of my child for new words and new tree-experiences. At the age of four he could identify practically every tree you could come across in the Dublin area, and not just the generic term — pine tree, say — but the individual species: Maritime pine, Scotch pine, Monterey pine, Stone pine, Austrian pine and so on. He recognised the trees at a distance of a hundred yards, as if by instinct, deciduous trees even in their leafless state in winter. A piece of twig with a bud on it was enough for him and in the end he could give you the name of a tree by the smell of its sawdust alone.

For years we went out into our surroundings as often as we could and always carried home firewood — we must have been a well-known sight, here in strait-laced suburbia, the father with some heavy logs on his shoulders, followed by a small fellow with a bundle of sticks, like a beast of burden driven by a child. Only that the ox in question, myself, was every bit as happy as the child, my driving force. For a time there was a phase when our tree-world even had a spiritual dimension. Near our house there stood a majestic old ash tree, with a ravaged crown but a magnificent trunk. For a while the boy visited that tree daily — 'Now I have to go to ash!' he used to announce; when there, he talked quietly to it — to Him? —and laid little offerings, usually flowers, at its mighty foot, with all the signs of veneration for a godhead.

Our ways, our walks, our talks, our whole life was all about trees — and gradually moments of near-madness began creeping into this monomania. One evening I returned home to the sight of my seven-year-old directing a JCB into our driveway. On its scoop lay an absolutely gigantic chunk from a beech tree, the lowest, most gnarled section, which the driver was about to lower down. Unable to split or saw this timber monstrosity with their power-tools, the workmen had intended to dump it before my son talked them into delivering it to our house — oh, he was totally irresistible in his obsession, I knew that only too well! The driver and myself, we both felt rather embarrassed when, regrettably, I had to cancel my son's tall order.

One Christmas matters came to a head. German parents traditionally decorate their Christmas trees as late as Christmas Eve, for the giving of presents on that same evening. I was occupied with this pleasant task when my wife came into the room, wide-eyed, and without saying a word pulled me out onto the road. There the pavement in front of our house was covered with a veritable mountain of Christmas trees, spilling over onto the roadway. The givers of this present were nowhere to be seen but I soon found out what had happened; it wasn't hard to guess. My son had seen that not all of the trees had been sold and had told the sellers that we wouldn't mind taking the rest. As we lived just around the corner, the offer was convenient for them, as it would save them the trip to the tip-head. So, gratefully, they accepted it and had delivered. What was there to do? I laughed my maddest laugh, and started to clear the road by shooting the trees over the wall into our front garden, counting them in the process — 189 Christmas trees — a figure *imprinted* on my memory — large and small, but mainly oversized ones. My little impresario stood by my side and proudly named them for me: Lodgepole pine! Douglas fir! Noble fir! Sitka spruce! Norway spruce! It was cold and dark, wet snowflakes were settling on the scene. I fought with a rising sense of exasperation, and came out victorious. It was Christmas, after all, and this mess had to be accepted as a present, an unexpected, uncalled-for, spiky, troublesome, labour-intensive one, but a Christmas present all the same! Joy to the World!

Among Primates

Some people one would prefer not to have had an influence on one's life. Ludwig Labert, for instance. I met him several times at different theatres during my acting career; each time he was just about to leave his job as dramatic adviser and director as I started mine as an actor. Ludwig never lasted long. He seemed interested in developing a closer relationship with me; I was not and thought I made that clear enough, but he still kept up the contact for more than a decade. On one occasion he was even instrumental in my getting the best engagement of my whole career; but then he was also instrumental in it not being renewed, through giving me some stupid advice which I was even more stupid to follow, against all my better instincts. That, in turn, had a most comprehensive effect on my whole existence — my marriage, my change of profession, my move to Ireland, my subsequent life here.

Ludwig would not have been my first choice for such a pivotal part in my biography. I didn't like him. It was not so much his physical appearance that antagonised me — his blond, curly hair, blond beard, baby-blue eyes and lips set in a permanent smile over long teeth. Or that he wore a cloak instead of a coat, and a beret rather than a cap or hat. Nothing wrong with all that, I suppose. Looking back now, I suspect the problem was his character which I perceived to be too worryingly close to my own. When I was still in school my German teacher had once cut my self-confidence to the quick by telling me coldly that I was a bluffer. That had hurt, and thenceforth I tried to make amends. But Ludwig, as I saw him, was all bluff, yet happily, proudly so. Bluff was his very element. He flaunted what I found my most embarrassing trait, my worst temptation and potential. Being near him, my unwished-for *doppelgänger*, raised my innermost hackles. So I kept a cool distance. Like myself he left the theatre, living for a while in London where he did some work for BBC radio and TV, before relocating in Vienna, a most fitting place for him, I'd venture to say. We never met again until a couple of years ago, and then in circumstances for which there is only one word: weird.

Early one Saturday morning I went with my young son to the zoo here in Dublin. We headed straight to the house of the big apes, the first visitors there. We had hardly entered the building when a friendly voice greeted us, in German, with '*Guten Tag!*'. We were pleasantly taken aback, but as there was nobody to be seen, we just vaguely mumbled *Guten Tag*. Apart from the animals, the place appeared to be completely empty. '*Guten Tag!*', the voice repeated charmingly, '*mein Name ist Ludwig Labert!*' I froze. Yes, I recognised Ludwig's well-groomed articulation, his honeyed tone. It was him. But where was he hiding? Was he playing a trick on me? Again we looked in all the corners — nobody, no blond beard, no black cloak. Next he intoned: '*Ich komme aus Deutschland!*' — 'I come from Germany!' I felt it sounded like a threat, by now the situation had become decidedly spooky. Had Ludwig lured me into some kind of Hitchcockian trap? For spite, for revenge? My conscience *vis-à-vis* him it seems, wasn't the clearest. But why here, and what part did the apes play in his game? They were lying in a relaxed huddle, heads lolling, arms dangling — no Ludwig among them. Then I noticed how some of them were looking up at a box fixed in the top left-hand corner of their cage — they were watching TV, educational TV, a BBC German language course. And Ludwig Labert, the famous dandy, had just introduced himself to the gorillas. Using his own name in the programme, the conceited git, for posterity.

I was delirious, a big wave of *schadenfreude* lifted me up and carried me away, I danced with glee. 'What's wrong?' asked my son. 'Nothing, nothing!' I giggled, and tried to explain. But as I did, it dawned on me that what Ludwig had done a moment ago was aping *me*, in my daily work as a language teacher. Had he, or rather his electronic self, caught me out, or I him? Who had the last laugh? I found it impossible to untangle that one, and gave up. And then we went and talked to the little monkeys.

Happy Sad

It's of little use trying to explain the beauty of the air hostess on our flight from Ireland to Malta; suffice it to say that my wife, too, was struck by her charm, so there must have been something beyond everyday heterosexual attraction. Beyond her full, wavy, black hair, gathered at the back, her face softly but firmly modelled and her warm and ready smile that really seemed to mean it, though not without a faint hint of amusement around her lovely, dark eyes. One might have called it an idealised Mediterranean face, combining the warmth of the sunlight and the pleasing mystery of the evening shade — but there I go, trying to describe the indescribable. After all, it is always something about people, rather than just their looks, that seems to contain the secret of their beauty.

She appeared not really to be part of the environment she shared with us, the passengers, in a bullet-shaped thing flying south, as if she was here only by chance and, being her own gentle self, was helping with the job at hand, dispensing the meals and her graceful smiles like gifts to us. In between she sometimes just stood there, looking contentedly inwards, as if she was thinking of some joy-filled place from which she had come as a messenger among us. If that sounds as if there was something otherworldly about this young woman, nothing could be further from the truth; if anything she appeared more sensually and sensitively real than anybody else on the plane.

While the three of us were occupied with the usual things, meals and magazines, all the time, unobtrusively, keeping an eye on 'our' hostess, the pilot suddenly announced, with a modicum of excitement in his voice, that we should look out to our left for an interesting view. We all did — and were overwhelmed: we were crossing the Alps which lay largely invisible under a thick cloud-cover, shimmering like mother-of-pearl in pinks and greys in the slanted light of the setting sun. But out of this infinity of cloud jutted a number of jagged, blindingly white peaks, like wolves' teeth, menacing, aiming for the thin metal skin of our container, even if some 20,000 feet below us. It was frightening, you felt the threat cold on your own skin. At the same time the vista was breathtakingly beautiful in its sunset-coloured immensity. We all gasped and murmured, and only reluctantly turned our faces away when the sight slowly sank away behind us. As my little family settled back into our seats there was the air hostess standing beside us, who with a serene smile asked us the strangest, most perplexing question I'd ever been faced with — 'Well, are you happy now or sad?'

I was at a loss for words and blushed, stuttering something like: 'Oh, very, very happy!', but immediately felt the hopeless inadequacy of my reply. I had just been high above the highest mountains of the Continent, I had seen the planet in its raw inhumanity, a sight as homely and hospitable as the pictures we see of the barren wastes of the moon and Mars — how could one be happy looking at that? Yet how dare you be sad, either, having been shown your place in the universe lit by such silent grandeur? There was no answer to her question, the question itself was the answer. Maybe happy and sad are not mutually exclusive, maybe they are inseparably wrapped into each other? Maybe I should have answered: Both! With a simple question our messenger had lifted us lightly into a realm beyond simple words.

Meanwhile the plane was hurtling down the western coast of the Italian peninsula. Looking out towards the east, we saw the sky cloaked in deep blue-black, while at the same time, on the western side, the setting sun created a glorious spectacle of orange and red. For a few minutes, the plane was travelling down the dividing line between night and day, darkness and light — or was it happy and sad? But soon night took over, and below us the surface of the earth displayed its own constellations, the cities we passed over sparkling like the Milky Way. The planet was showing off; Rome — a lake of lights, Naples likewise, then the ink-black sea, some Sicilian fireworks and then, close already, the winding street-lights, the straight landing-lights of Malta. We had arrived.

At the exit door our hostess waited and, with a graceful wave and a smile, presented us with this other island. A swell of warm, dry air enveloped us, with a strange, new, spicy scent, as we stepped out of our time-capsule back down into the happy sad world.

Blue Bird Blues

Botanically and archaeologically our two weeks on Malta had been more than rewarding — in spring the three rocky islands of the Maltese archipelago are ablaze with wildflowers, just like Ireland's own limestone area, the Burren, and just as in the latter, there are archaeological remains virtually everywhere. But at that time I was in the heyday of my bird-watching passion, and on that count our visit had been a disappointment, considering that the islands are situated along one of the main routes of bird migration between Europe and Africa. They are also literally studded with hides for the island's 25,000 inveterate bird-hunters, which explains the paucity of bird life there. Nevertheless there had been two memorable moments; I had both heard and seen the secretive blue rock thrush, a bird of the wildest, most inaccessible places, whose flutey, wistful song echoes from the cliff-faces. It's a relative of our blackbird, but the plumage is blue, a soft, dusty blue, from beak to tail. You have to be really lucky or very patient to get a glimpse of the blue rock thrush as it flits from cover to cover.

The other sighting, also of a predominantly blue bird, had been sensational in comparison; out in the sun-drenched central plain an electrically blue flash had dazzled my eye for a moment, before I realised this had been a bird swooping down from its perch on a telegraph pole; a roller, perhaps the most beautiful bird of our continent, if only for the open, generous way in which he shows his glorious colours, the blue flash of the wings signalling his presence all around, to his own kind and also, unfortunately, to mine. Because of his coloration, the roller has always been sought after by trophy hunters and in Western Europe it is only an occasional straggler now. This sighting alone had compensated for all the uneventful days.

It was our last afternoon on Malta when, taking a quiet farewell stroll through the fields and gardens near our hotel and coming round a dense bush, we suddenly found ourselves face to face with a small, elderly, wiry, brown man armed with an enormous shotgun. The shock was mutual, but it immediately dissolved into friendliness and laughter. He was out pigeon-shooting he said, and where did we come from? When we told him we were Germans living in Ireland, he had nothing but praise for both nations. He himself had been living for 30 years in Sheffield, England, he had raised a family there, had seen his children marry and move away, and had been widowed two years ago. Since then he had returned to his home island, building himself a nice villa in town and a little summer-house out here, to spend his time gardening, fishing and pigeon-shooting. Most of his sentences ended in a burst of laughter, and while we were walking together he picked sweet broad beans here and loquats there and presented them to us — he was happy in his skin, this was his domain, and he shared of its riches with open hands.

Eventually the white cube of a house appeared between the lemon trees and the bamboo — his summer-house. He invited us in; we were delighted. The house consisted basically of one large room decorated with all the paraphernalia to be expected in a staunchly Catholic country: pictures of saints and popes, the Cross, the statues, family photographs, plastic flowers. But all that I only took in later, for my first glance around stunned me into speechlessness; from all the four walls glassy eyes peered at us — stuffed birds, dozens of them. I recognised purple heron, night heron, hen harrier — all of them rare, all strictly protected. And there, too, was my blue rock thrush, hunched in a posture of eternal furtiveness, collecting dust on its dusty-blue feathers. And, of course, taking pride of place, there too was a roller, spreading its lovely wings, but no flash, just a stiff parading of now lifeless splendour. What a deadly little zoo we found ourselves in!

But here was our friendly host again, carrying glasses filled to the rim with a welcoming drink. Cheers! I said how impressed I was with his collection, trying to sound neutral, non-censoring. He laughed and said: Ah, that's nothing! You should see what I have in my townhouse! And that again is nothing compared with the collections some of my friends have built up over the years! And he laughed, again. I managed to mumble that I much preferred to see the birds through my binoculars, and alive. He laughed: And I like to shoot them! More laughter.

There we stood, eye to eye and smile to smile, two men who never, ever would comprehend each other's instincts and emotions. What was there to say? We shared another drink and a few more laughs, and then we all had to leave, we for our flight home, he for some more — pigeon-shooting. When we looked back, he was still standing at his gate, waving, laughing, a small man with a big gun.

An Early, Early Show

Our plane had arrived late in Rome by several hours. The brakelights of the last airport bus faded into the dark. Then squabbles over the few available taxis. When at last we made it to Stazione Termini we found that the hotel in which our Dublin travel agent had booked us a room for the night had ceased operating years ago. All the other *pensiones* around the station were *'completo'*. And by now it was half-past-one in the morning. Time to count our blessings. Yes, it could be worse, it could be cold and wet, for instance. Instead, although only Easter week, there was a balmy, summer breeze caressing the night. From Africa! we told ourselves. And the moon shone. Why not grasp the opportunity and camp out in the open? So the three of us — father, mother and eight-year-old son — settled down on the pavement in front of the by now chained and locked station — and soon realised that our little mishap had delivered us straight onto the stage of Rome's nocturnal street theatre, as dumb extras, as it were.

Despite the advanced hour, the broad pavement was still teeming with people, everybody moving about deliberately and with panache. On our left, Fortuna was being tested by a group of men throwing coins towards the station's glassy front. The coins thrown, they followed them casually, picking them up and doing something with them in a tight huddle. A sudden roar then rose from their midst, and back they went intently to the kerb, and the whole procedure started again, and again, right through the small hours, with the same relaxed intensity, until finally they all dwindled into the dawn.

In the shadows on our right some ancient ruins were looming; at their foot a number of Rome's street-people, men and women, had come together around a blazing fire which they fed with cardboard boxes and scrap timber. They were drinking, shouting and singing, then one by one falling asleep. From time to time one or another of them would steal away and relieve him- or herself a few steps away, the breeze from that direction brought with it wafts of smoke, of wine and of urine, the eternal smells of the Eternal City.

Thus the gamblers and the down-and-outs occupied the wings of our stage, while in between, that is, in front of us, the nighthawks were on patrol. One of them, a tall, long-haired fellow, dangerous looking like a slim blade, but also pale and beautiful, like a Caravaggio Christ, strutted past us and, pausing for just a moment, stretched out his arm in a gesture of blessing towards my young son and calmly intoned: *Dormire*! — Sleep! That was fine, but the bloke who followed was a different matter; bulky, drunk, unshaven, with bloodshot eyes under bushy eyebrows, he crawled towards us, a dark figure, a Judas Iscariot if ever there was one. I fingered for my pocket-knife, ready for mortal combat, as he crouched down in front of my precious child, his hairy paw making slowly for the uneasy little face. And then a deep moan rose from the fiend's chest: *Ah*! *Bambino biondo*! *Que bello*! He fondled the blond cap of hair and insisted he would buy him a Coca Cola. But everything was closed at this hour, so he settled for a big kiss, with pursed lips, on the child's forehead and staggered away disconsolately.

Next on the scene was a cardinal, no less. In full regalia, purple frock and skull-cap, bearded too, and walking barefoot in sandals. A slight, lively figure, he tripped from group to group, gradually gathering a retinue of young men around him. Was he walking the path of virtue or of vice? Not an easy thing to know with Roman cardinals, past or present, fake or otherwise. In the end, they all got into a number of taxis, and away they went.

Then, all of a sudden, an outburst of pure passion! At first it seemed merely the hysterical fit of a dishevelled, heavily made-up young woman, yet one that built into a long and impressively sustained scene. She strode along the whole width of the station's front, screaming her pain and indignation into the night air, up to the moon, while the cause and object of her emotionalism followed a few steps behind her, a bony individual, limping badly with the help of a crutch, and punctuating her cadenzas at regular intervals with resounding expletives in a deep baritone voice. Their duet appeared simultaneously rehearsed and spontaneous; frightening and hilarious, it was the stuff operas are made of, the Great Sexual Drama, and it did not fail to attract cheers and appreciation from the bystanders, until the two protagonists ran out of steam and made off, together, for their place of rest.

A huge, brick-red sun had risen from the roofs of Rome. The stage was empty; the gamblers, the players, the actors and those who didn't bother anymore, all had exited. The station was being unlocked, the day-folk were crowding in, and soon the three of us were on our way, speeding through the unmysterious, blinding brightness of an Italian spring morning, looking forward to seeing familiar faces.

Talking Bull-Manure

The sliding door of my compartment opened, and a man entered for whom I felt a spontaneous dislike. I had reserved for myself a nice window-seat on the train from Berlin to Hamburg, and he, of course, sat down directly opposite me — a fleshy, compact figure with a shockingly repulsive face, small, slanted eyes, tightly combed-back hair from a low brow, and a callous expression around his heavy jaw. Concentration-camp guard — that was the first association that came to my mind. We remained the only passengers in our compartment. I dreaded the hours I would have to spend confronting this face, and hastily fumbled for my news magazine, intending to avoid any contact.

I say these nasty things about a fellow human being in a gesture of public remorse. A conversation I'd had shortly before this encounter in the train should have prepared me better for it. On the occasion of her retrospective exhibition in Dublin I had asked a famous painter, praised in particular for her sensitive portraits, why she had stopped painting them in recent years. Marie-Louise von Motesiczky, then in her eighties, had answered: 'Oh, you know, one can't really see anything truthful in the faces of people!' And she had added what basically we all know; that mass murderers look like bank-clerks, bank-clerks like poets and poets like serial killers, and vice versa. Not to mention the obvious lack of truth in all the made-up faces.

My mass-murderous opposite in the train to Hamburg soon struck up a conversation; I yielded, ever more readily, and was rewarded with a pleasant and instructive journey through the rather boring, flat, wooded northern part of the former GDR, the man's homeland. This was a few years before the fall of the regime, and he had been given permission to visit relatives in West Germany. He was looking forward to his stay there with childlike trepidation and curiosity, and he also showed a considerable sense of humour and irony when talking about his life in an LPG, a *Landwirtschaftliche Produktionsgenossenschaft*, the basic unit of the former GDR's agricultural system. And in passing he taught me that, just as with people, one shouldn't take words at face value either, not even the most obvious ones.

Every LPG, within the planned economy of the socialist state, had its assigned task; one was responsible for growing vegetables, another for fruit or cereals and so on. My man's LPG was breeding cattle. And of course, they kept bulls.

Now, as naturally as the market system creates waste, the planned economy creates shortages, all kinds of shortages, but in the context of this story, it is shortages in spare parts that are relevant. To cope with these shortages a secret but generally known bartering system, a genuine market mechanism, had developed. Every LPG took great care to collect and store items that were of possible demand among suppliers of, say, tractor spare parts. In the case of my man's LPG, the most precious commodity they had to offer on this underground market was, wait for it, *Bullenmist*, bull-manure. Bullshit was the sesame that opened many a door and gave access to many a hoard of hard-to-come-by spare parts. The fruit- and vegetable-growing LPGs would give their little fingers for it.

Now, I assume it wasn't just a male-chauvinist myth that made this by-product of the bulls more valued than that of the poor cows — in order to enhance the quality of the bulls' performance, they were probably given richer food which in turn resulted in a better-quality manure. Be that as it may, the word 'bullshit' has since acquired for me a new, richer dimension. I have been enlightened, and I wince if somebody uses it, as sometimes happens, in a derogatory way.

My fellow-traveller's face, by the way, in the course of our exchanges, became ever more fascinating and appealing, especially when he laughed.

Noises, Sounds and Sweet Airs

Wearily I ascended the stairs from the underworld of the Underground; from a cacophony of hissing and rumbling, echoing announcements and the shuffling of hasty feet, I climbed into the light of a hot August forenoon, on a day later declared the hottest Berlin had known in this century. On this morning I felt a complete stranger in my hometown, tired and listless after a sleepless night. How the last 20 years in a quiet suburban cul-de-sac in Dublin had alienated me from the noisy reality of Berlin's city centre! Only the insomniac knows the terror even a single motor-car can induce in the early morning hours! First, from a vague distance, like a wasp closing in, the slow, threatening, relentless approach, culminating in the entire body of air out there in the canyon of the street reverberating with excessive energy, and then the gradual withdrawal of the metal beast, leaving behind the wreckage of sleep. There had been many cars outside my bedroom last night, and now I found myself, limp and in a foul humour, on a traffic island, and I didn't like what I was confronted with; a tempest of vehicles encircling the island, a barrage of noise, glaring light, fumes and heat, and right before me the arrogant building of the KaDeWe, the 'Supermarket of the West', that cathedral of St Affluence, Berlin's answer to Harrods of London. Bad signals all around, I felt.

But there was also something else in the air, a friendlier message, though it took me a moment or two before I heard it — a pleasant, soothing sound, sweet and refreshing like skeins of spray from a waterfall or high fountain. Yes, it was music, but from where did it emanate? The island seemed to be full of it; it hovered above the roar of the traffic like larksong. Where was the musician? If, indeed, there was one at all? Ah yes, now I got a glimpse of him, half-hidden he stood among shrubs and flowering roses, a tall, skinny young man, playing a xylophone. Or was it the other way round — was it playing him? For he seemed to be completely possessed by and surrendered to it, his body bent over the keyboard like a cat about to leap, his arms flailing the air, his hands only a blur, like hummingbird wings. The tunes he played, though still recognisable, were wrapped in or, rather, dissolved in showers of trills and glissandi, every note disintegrating into sub-particles like a drop of water into a multitude of tiny droplets, creating a mist of sound you could almost breathe.

Swept along by the throng of pedestrians I crossed the road, but once safely on the other side, on the mainland as it were, I stopped again and looked back. The musician was invisible now, having disappeared in the shifting jigsaw of flowers, crowds and cars, in the hectic rush and general madness of the place. And rightly so, I felt, as if the charged atmosphere of this environment had expressed and purified itself through him, entering into every pore of his body and making it the medium, the instrument of transformation; what had only been undirected, raw energy, material aggression, chaos, became a continuous stream of musical spiritedness — trembling, though, and not at all of the same unshakeable substance as the background roar. And I felt I had partaken in that transformation, because here I stood, an ill-tempered, heavy-footed Caliban only moments ago, yet now 'the clouds methought would open and show riches, ready to drop upon me', as I closed my eyes and held my face into the drizzle of sweet airs, the element into which the airy spirit Ariel over there on his traffic island was liberating himself.

Not for long, of course, as the place which had given rise to such an experience was not exactly conducive to enjoying it, and there were also other sounds, alluring sounds, competing with the xylophonic enchantment. This time the music I heard came from afar, from a different time, a different land. At my back, at a distance from the traffic, was a street café with white tables and comfortable chairs in the dappled shadow of plane trees. The people who sat there, casually chatting and sipping summer drinks, were granted the extra luxury of musical entertainment, free of charge, unless, of course, they felt like dipping into their pockets; three buskers, one accordion, two guitars, were winding their way among the tables, turning to each other, turning to their audience, stopping here or there for a few bars, then again taking up the slow dancing steps of their tune, a tango — a lazy river of song meandering around summery islands. Across the road, the boy with the xylophone, he was the Here and Now, the ecstatic self-exhaustion of the Western world — but there, under the plane trees, a different tune was being played, a relaxed, sensual, Mediterranean or possibly Eastern European tune. There was an Old World gypsy charm about the three in their dark suits — yes, despite the merciless heat they wore white shirts and old-fashioned, dark, well-worn suits, though no ties. And the song they played was of the same sun-tanned, black-curled, weathered vintage as they were themselves. In fact, it was the main reason for my fascinated lingering. I had not heard it for, oh, maybe 30 or 40 years, though I had sometimes hummed it to myself. It brought me right back to my early childhood, in the years just after the War.

In those years Germans had indulged in a wave of Italian, or maybe only Italianate, pop music. The old German longing for the south, for a freer, fuller way of life may have been behind that, offering as it did an escape route from a dreary present to a romantic, warm and tuneful distance. And the most successful of these songs, played by the radio day in, day out, and whistled, hummed and sung by everyone I knew, was now being played by the three foreign buskers on Wittenbergplatz in the midday heat, 'The Fishermen of Capri'.

For me, of course, the song had no escapist connotations and the erotic element in it I probably missed altogether, but I liked the tune and a couple of verbal images in the lyrics — the red sun submerging in the sea, the pale sickle of the moon, the fishermen casting their nets 'in a wide arc' and, most of all, the men 'singing their timeless song from boat to boat' — oh, it was a very distant and purely poetic world which stole its way into my real one, where there were dangers from unexploded bombs and ammunition, warnings against deranged people who killed children, and the constant threat from epidemics such as typhoid fever and polio. These latter threats caused the mass evacuation of Berlin's children to the countryside, and that's how I spent a most wonderful summer in a small and remote Thuringian village. It took us three arduous days to get there — a journey of a couple of hours by car nowadays.

This again was a different world to the one I knew, but it was excitingly real. The village had a timeless pastoral air about it, there was not a single house in ruins, no scarcity of food, and there were the animals, goats and geese mainly, patient, and sometimes mysteriously impatient play-pals for the eight-year-old dreamer and outsider from the broken capital which, in my perception, was now a very distant place, in a life that, for the moment, I had left far behind.

However, after a few days in this other world, my host-parents switched on the radio one evening, and what did I hear? Yes, 'The Fishermen of Capri'. I can still feel my shock of disbelief, and I'm still unable to figure out clearly why I was so shaken. Was it that my sense of space and distance was suddenly confused? That I was confronted with the smallness of the world, just as I was coming to terms with its immensity? Or was it the unwelcome intrusion of technology into the realm of my imagination? A notion that nothing is what it appears to be, no matter how innocently and strongly we feel about it?

Whatever it was — I was deeply disappointed. I had travelled a thousand miles, only to arrive where I had left. And now, so many years later, as I listened to the song again, the same slight existential dizziness came over me: somewhere in the vastness of Eastern Europe the song with all those memories attached to it had weathered the changing times, as on a magic island, and now here it was again, as young and enticing as ever, unlike myself. Only by now the three musicians, having finished their work in the café, had rounded a corner, and so their music had trickled away like water in dry sand. And that's how I felt — stranded, though, at the same time, also refreshed and confirmed by my encounter, on wings of song, with my own self. And so I too ambled on.

It did not take me long before I reached the heart of what used to be West Berlin, the monumental ruin of the Kaiser-Wilhelm-Memorial Church, surrounded nowadays by a spacious pedestrian area. Here is a meeting-place for all inner-city life, especially around a bulging fountain made of flesh-coloured granite, the 'meatball', as the Berliners irreverently call it. It actually symbolises the globe itself, populated by a host of bronze creatures, human, demon and animal, and it spurts, sprays and exudes water from an amazing variety of apertures. Here city pigeons come for a sip and dogs for a splash, here children won't listen and tourists, exhausted by their video-recorders and plastic bags, slump down, close their eyes and listen to the sounds of water and cars in motion. And to music, because here it was that I had my third absorbing encounter with street music, within a shorter time span than it now takes to recount them. Barely audible among all the other noises I could just make out the voice of a single saxophone, playing jazz.

Looking for the origin of that voice I came across the following edifice: on one of the many mushroom-shaped granite benches which the global fountain had sprouted in its vicinity stood a white camping stool — the flimsy, collapsible sort, with a floppy canvas seat. But instead of soft canvas this stool had a short, white, wooden board. Placed on it was the cut-off from a wavin-pipe, maybe eight inches in diameter. It was jerking nervously to and fro on the short, white board. What kept it from falling off was another short board that lay on top of it, combining with it to make a little see-saw. And on the see-saw, his feet placed on either end, stood a young man in black jeans and a white vest, his sunburnt forehead and short, shiny hair crowned by some contraption, holding a tiny parasol over him as symbolic protection against the booming noonday sun. So, once again, from the bottom up: granite bench — camping stool — see-saw — musician — parasol. I was looking at the artist as *artiste*; he not only presented a balancing act of considerable daring, but also played music while doing so, and not badly at all! The saxophone hung from his neck as he played with both hands. His body was bent forward in a posture of extreme alertness, so it looked as if the notes were being hatched in the hollow of his body, then released through his lips into the shining body of the instrument. His feet, meanwhile, were incessantly at play on the see-saw, darting left and right and up and down, while his fingers fluttered over the keys. Now and again his right hand would suddenly fly out into the air, like the commanding gesture of a public speaker; for a moment you were shocked, afraid of being addressed by him, of becoming involved; but then you realised it was the arm movement of one in danger of losing his balance, his struggle against the force of gravity. The left hand meantime played on, until the right one was ready to join it again.

He played well — would he have played even better had he been standing on safe ground? But who would have paid him any attention then? Even as things stood, he was not exactly enjoying the limelight; few people threw him a glance, even fewer dropped a coin into the crumpled cap on the pavement in front of his shaky little tower of song. Competition was avid here: over there I could see the three Capri Fishermen arriving, the twanging of a barrel-organ was also audible; a whole cooperative of portrait painters, six of them, working in six different styles, represented the claims of the visual arts on the public's attention and purse; there was also begging and cheating, selling and thieving going on; the presence of drugs could be sensed and seen — and from the high cliff of the Europa Centre the true giants of competition looked down on all of us: Mitsubishi, Samsung, MacDonalds, Coca Cola and, from the very top, the star of the occident, Mercedes-Benz.

Suddenly I felt utterly humbled by, and full of admiration for, this young man's courage. He truly earned an honest crust, by the sweat of his brow. Or was it only arrogance, excessive pride in his own prowess that had driven him up there? Or desperation? And how, indeed, did he manage to get on top of this trembling construction? How would he get down from his high perch without risking life and limb? Inept in practical matters as I am, I could not imagine a way of achieving those tricks. Instead I stared, transfixed, at this monument to artistic bravery and daring. Was not every artist caught up forever in his or her own tight-rope act; vying for public attention and, at the same time, dreading, even despising it, always having to weigh the public's expectations against the demands of the artistic conscience, always trying to remain true to the inner voice, while also trying to make a living? And was not *balance* the secret of all human enterprise, the task, even, of every single day? Was I not seeing there a momentary monument to all of us, to our continuous endeavour not to lose our equilibrium, while trying to give of our best?

Fortunately, before I got too high myself, I was brought down to earth by a beggar who asked me for a light or, alternatively, a deutschmark. While I was fumbling in my pockets, the saxophone suddenly fell silent, and I just managed to get a glimpse of the smooth dismantling of the monument. It was so quick and simple — it's almost embarrassing to tell; one hand kept holding the instrument, the other shot down and released one leg by replacing its pressure on the see-saw, that leg stepped down onto the granite, and that was it. The artiste gathered his props, donned his cap, and then dumbfounded, I saw my vision of artistic high-mindedness, my Orpheus, enveloped by a swirl of disinterested spirits, descend into the underworld of the Underground.

Facing The Gate

Exhausted from walking in the heat and dust of Berlin's newly liberated and united centre, I sat on a bench near the Brandenburg Gate. I was surrounded there by smells and sights of a specifically Berlin nature; curried fried sausages enriched the air, the bustle of the souvenir market entertained the eye. Remnants from a barely bygone time were on sale: concrete lumps from the fallen Wall, uniform items from the former People's Army. Plus artefacts in darkly glowing colours from the far ends of Eastern Europe, Russian dolls and lacquered boxes, Polish carvings. And reams and reams of picture postcards. The Gate lay there, honey-coloured and dozing in the sunshine; its fetters fallen from it, it breathed again and, as nothing new had as yet been built in its proximity, there was plenty of breathing space for it, and us.

I tried to look at it with a detached and curious eye, I wanted to figure out what it was that made it the one landmark the city of Berlin is identified with all over the world; why it is the one edifice all the political systems for more than 200 years have used and abused in making it the centrepiece of their self-presentation, to the people of Germany and to the rest of the world.

Compared to other buildings of similar international stature, it is not particularly large or imposing. Like all structures in the classical mode it has pleasing dimensions; it does not overwhelm or intimidate. At the same time it reaches out well beyond our physical limitations, toward the loftiness of our ideals, the most basic ones, peace, justice, the joy of living. Seen obliquely it can appear massive and cluttered, but if you approach it frontally, as it is designed to be, on the avenue leading to and through it, its exquisite gracefulness becomes apparent and truly heart-stirring. Because of the distances involved, every approach, even by car, is a slow one; as the image grows on you, a festive expectancy arises and is ultimately fulfilled. The vertical and horizontal lines, support and weight, are so perfectly balanced, the tension between the emotional restraint of the Gate itself and the exuberance of the Quadriga on its top so satisfying — the mind simply relaxes in an experience of utter rightness. Maybe, I thought, that simple 'rightness' is the secret of the Brandenburg Gate, the message that makes it so universally attractive and acceptable.

I was just about losing the ground under my feet in my mulling over the Brandenburg Gate, when something happened before my eyes that brought me back, with a shock, to the level of the street; a teenage gypsy girl — black-haired, brown-skinned, poorly but colourfully dressed, very thin, a slip of a girl — had approached two young German men, tall, strong-looking fellows, with denims covering their swelling bellies. She handed them a little note, no doubt with a plea for money written on it. But they, rather than giving her the cold shoulder which, I suppose, would have been their right, in a totally unprovoked show of aggressiveness, had grabbed that piece of paper from her, thrown it on the ground and trampled on it — a gesture of outrage totally, ridiculously disproportionate to the occasion. Arms swung back next, threatening to slap her face. The girl recoiled in fright and withdrew, and the two heroes strutted off, obviously convinced they had the tacit approval of everyone around, of having done a service to the public. And perhaps they had, for nobody said anything, nor did I myself intervene in any way.

The here and now had shown its colours, and the future too. Berlin was teeming with foreigners of all kinds; the atmosphere was tense. The girl had been attacked as a woman and as a pauper, but primarily as a foreigner, as somebody who looked and acted differently. In front of the Brandenburg Gate which I had just endowed with such a spiritual aura and right-setting effect! I had, for a moment forgotten that they are two completely different things: the lofty Gate and the endless street that runs through it.

A Tourist Trap

The city centre of Berlin is awash with monuments and memorials; warriors sporting muscles and bellies and beards, thinkers presenting dignity and noble profiles; there is the Victory Column, shimmering with gilded cannon barrels, with a winged goddess on top as if forever stuck on a launching pad; there are, from more recent times, the sad little crosses for those who tried to get over the Wall and were killed in the attempt, almost all of them terribly young, many nameless; and there will be, sooner or later, a monument to the Holocaust. So much, often questionable, glory, and how much suffering and shame — the air around the throngs of tourists winding their way from one memorial site to the next is filled with the soundless cries of invisible victors and their victims. Monuments are like boulders in the flow of people and of time, trying to arrest it, at least for a brief moment of commemoration, through the evocative presence of crafted bronze, or stone, or steel. But recently I came across a memorial in my hometown which achieved the same result by being made of the flimsiest of all possible building materials, by being made entirely — of absence.

I was strolling across Bebel Square off Unter den Linden, Berlin's O'Connell Street, if you like. The square is bordered on four sides by the very bastions of civilisation: the University, the Opera House, the Catholic Cathedral and the former National Library, with its inscription '*Nutrimentum Spiritus*' spelling out what this ambience is meant to be all about: the nourishment of the mind.

I had lifted my eyes to the tops of those buildings from where classical heroes, gods, muses and personified virtues, blackened by the smoke of peace and war, exhort the citizenry to do the Good and the Right and the Proper. I was looking up with particular pleasure at the ladies among them, their half-clad poses of high morality, when suddenly my feet sensed a difference underfoot: the rough pebble pavement had given way to a hard, smooth, ringing surface. When I looked down, I almost leapt back with the shock, for I was standing, as on thin ice, on a five-foot square of glass, looking down into a room, 15 feet or so below, painted entirely white and receiving its light from above, from where I stood. What's more, this chamber, or vault, was completely empty but for the equally white shelves running around its four walls. And it was the bareness of those shelves that created the second, lingering, slow-burning shock. No inscriptions, no explanations that I could see from where I stood. You had to work it out all for yourself.

It was on this perfidiously selected spot where, on May 10th 1933, Joseph Goebbels, with the enthusiastic support of professors and students from the university across the street, had launched the action 'Fighting the Un-German Spirit'. Some 20,000 books were burnt here, books by, among many others, Albert Einstein, Thomas Mann, Franz Kafka and, of course, Heinrich Heine, Germany's first great Jewish writer who, a hundred years earlier, had predicted that where books are burnt, human beings would soon follow.

How to commemorate that event, that monstrous act of negation, more fittingly, I had to agree, than with a 'negative monument'? One that does not dare rise into the air, but burrows into the common ground, awaiting to undercut the unsuspecting sightseer with a glimpse of the blinding void that lurks under the surface we all tread?

In the Middle of Life

He sits on the sunny forest floor and writes his initial with a short stick in the white dust between his outstretched legs. The earth underneath is darker, so the H, for Henry, is clearly inscribed. Then he sweeps his hand swiftly across the letter, and it disappears. 'Look!' he says to me, standing in front of him with a handful of wild raspberries, looking down at the radiant face of the little discoverer, 'Look! Now I'm here — and now I'm gone!' 'Yes, Henry, that is so,' I say, and feed him the raspberries.

We're on holiday here. He's my godchild, and this is the first time the two of us are together for such a long time, for two whole weeks. It's also the first time that he is away from his mother and that he is so deep in the countryside. He is a city child, six years old and due to start school in a few weeks' time. So I have the immense pleasure of experiencing his bright intelligence still in free, unclipped flight, his appetite for insight still insatiable, before they are institutionally regimented and numbed. 'I'm interested in everything except cars and food!' he had told me on the phone when I had inquired about his interests. No worry about entertainment then, but another worry stays with me day and night — the fear that he might come to some harm under my care. He is an only child, his father having died tragically soon after his birth. At night I lie awake and try to envisage every possible risk in our plans for the following day. Fortunately, in the light of day I relax, and we have all the things that boys of any age enjoy: camp-fires, bows and arrows, tree-houses, mystery tours. But the scene on the forest floor has touched a sore spot in my mind.

Our base is an isolated, old farmhouse in the middle of nowhere in the North German Plain — not an exciting landscape, but if, like Henry, you are interested in everything, there is plenty to discover. All of life is conveniently laid out around us. Wider and wider we draw the circles of our explorations and, true to his word, his mind engages with everything. The area is rich in historical remains; there is a huge double ring-fort in what feels like primeval forest, and a number of impressive megalithic monuments. 'Stone Age, Bronze Age, Iron Age — when was the Wood Age?' he asks. That's a relatively easy one to answer, but what about: 'Where are the Stone Age people now?' How to convey to a child that they are dead and buried under their megaliths, and at the same time still alive and kicking under our 21st-century skins? I was struggling there, but my efforts to do justice to 'Where do human beings come from?' are rewarded with an excited cry of recognition: 'So, then people are nature too, just like animals and plants!' Yes, yes, Henry, but many find this hard to understand. But, then, he himself has already realised: 'The most difficult thing is, to know what you don't know!'

In the evenings it is story-telling time. As he slowly grows quiet and sleepy, a precious silence descends on us. I sit by his bedside, see the golden-shimmering down on his temples, and see his mother, many years ago, and ponder the strange ways joy and pain have repeatedly given birth to each other over all those years. And once, in one of those peaceful, pre-sleep moments, he says, from out of his own pondering: 'Peter, I'm glad that I'm somebody who I like to be.' And so am I, Henry. Very glad.

On our last day we pay our farewell visit to the lake, where we've had so much fun in these blistering two weeks. This time I leave him alone for a few minutes, with his bare-handed channel-digging, and swim out into the lake, to stretch my muscles and dive down to the emerald water-plants. But soon, conscientiously, I turn back and see him wading into the water to meet me. Presently, our two beaming faces are floating towards each other on the water's surface like two happy ducks. When the distance between us is, maybe, ten yards, I see a tiny wavelet leaping up at his mouth and entering it. He gulps, confused, and loses his foothold. And swallows again. And founders. And I see him drown, before my eyes — no, of course not, I'm too near for that, but in the few seconds it takes me to reach him, I see the little face go through all the stages of drowning; first, the sudden change from delight to confusion and terror, then the will to struggle, to fight against the enfolding forces, and then, as the mind realises the overwhelming power of the element seeking him, the surrender, the acceptance, the head sinking sideways, the eyes closed as if for sleep and peace. But at that moment, of course, after a few terrified strokes, I'm there, and yank him from the clutches of the dark, and heave him onto my shoulder. He hasn't lost consciousness; he is spluttering and coughing a bit and, almost immediately, still on my shoulder, he stammers: 'I'll never do that again!' And in the same breath: 'We shan't tell Mummy about that!'

As I lie, shuddering, on the beach, my face in the cool, objective smell of moist sand, I slowly come to understand how that is all, that there is really nothing more to be said. A moment ago, our world was shaking in its foundations. Now it is solid again, held together by the rational, loving words risen from the depth of a young human soul.

Caught in a Heat Wave

This big Continental city is sweltering in a heat wave. I'm a visitor here, a sightseer for a few days. I'm in my hotel room now, my mind buzzing with images of journey and arrival, of the first hectic hours here. It's late in the evening, and I'm tired, hoping for sleep. But the room is a cube of warm, stagnant air; I lie naked on the bed, restless, sleepless. To escape the welter of images in my mind I turn on the TV, zapping between dozens of stations. That's worse than my inner programme, so I deliver myself back to it. Midnight is approaching, it's dark now outside. My room has access to a large, unkept roof-terrace. Maybe some fresh air can be found there, some calm. But it's only the stale city breath that receives me, and more disquiet; blinking airplanes, ambulance sirens, shouts and screams from the clientele of the many bars and restaurants down below; on two sides the terrace is bordered by street-canyons, a vertical drop of eight floors — vertigo makes a grab for my stomach; weakening, I withdraw from the edge to the wall at the back, lean against its harsh, warm surface, waiting. For what?

A strange, slightly mysterious sight catches my eye: the house opposite has a small penthouse perched on its roof, like the tabernacle on an altar. I look into a short corridor that leads to a tiny room bathed in a pale light, the kitchen, it would seem. There, a thin old man sits on a chair in his underwear, in a strained, upright position; one foot is hoisted on top of the table in front of him where, out of my sight, someone seems to be tending to it. For a few minutes I watch, but when nothing else happens, my attention wanders and I return to the seething solitude of my own room.

As I open the window, a draft leaps up like a roused animal, blowing the long, light curtains horizontally into the room, a huge, soundless sail, flapping, billowing, and carrying me away — I finally doze off. Minutes later the couple next door arrive and immediately turn on their TV; plastic voices, in a staccato of foreign tongues, and canned laughter seep through the wall. Maybe they want to camouflage their love-making, I think, and bury my head in the pillow. Hours later, as dawn breaks, I can hear the end-of-program signal pipping and realise that for my neighbours a blaring TV is a precondition for sleep. I both curse and envy them. Then another day in the blistering streets, and another evening in my hotel room. Nothing has changed: the heat, my restlessness, the escape onto the terrace, the exhausted city air. What am I doing here, running around all day, only to end up, my back against a wall, looking at an ocean of roofs?

But tonight I must have come out a few minutes earlier, for this time the enigmatic scene in the penthouse across the road is only about to begin. I had completely forgotten the bony old man, who today is still standing or, rather, skipping from one foot to the other, lifting his knees in a sort of slow, pained Rumpelstilsken dance. Presently an old woman in her nightgown crosses the scene and disappears; the man sits down, lifts his foot onto the table, and yesterday's half-visible ceremony takes its course — is it a massage, the dressing of a wound, the soothing of a chronic pain? In any case, it's a

Samaritan deed, you can see the relief in the old man's upturned face. I realise that what I'm witnessing is a nightly ritual, the concluding act of all their days together; and for a moment the whole city, the feverish night sky, all the unfocused agitation around me, and in me — all seem centred around and arrested by what I'm watching in the luminous little cell over there, unreachably near, on the other side of the street.

His treatment over, the old man gets up and, still limping, walks into the corridor, in my direction, and turns off into what must be their bedroom. He is soon followed by the old woman, with firm, flat-footed steps; for a second I can make out the outline of a heavy body under her light nightdress; then, with a shock, I see her heading straight towards me. I freeze, wishing to melt into the wall. Now, at the window, she raises her hand, as if in greeting — and I react in the most primitive fashion: I turn my head away; if I can't see her, she can't see me! Then I tell myself that I shouldn't worry, that from her bright room she can't look into my darkness, but when I turn my face back, she is gone; the curtains are drawn, the lights switched off; another of their days is done, soon they will sleep.

A word rises in me, from the bottom of the night, from the sediment of my mind, where it had sunk, unmissed, unused for, oh, for decades. A word, uncomfortable to utter, with a harsh sound like a stone crushed accidentally between your teeth, a word with sharp, shimmery edges. Sacrament.

The Hiring Fair

I'm early, as usual, my compulsive German punctuality unbroken after all those years in Ireland. But there is the 'Casting' sign, so I'm in the right place. On my return, after lying for a few minutes on the grass in a nearby park, I find the waiting-room is already packed with middle-aged actresses. Most of them know each other — embraces and kisses, compliments and camaraderie make the awful awareness of head-to-head competition more bearable. At the same time, of course, silent mutual assessment — looks are so important, aren't they? But what exactly is required today? Some of the women have come in casual attire, others are carefully dressed and made up, their demeanour, too, in all shades, between jolly and formally stiff.

The first of them is called into the audition-room. She soon reappears, flushed, as we will all be after our few minutes with the director. She's aghast; credible typewriting skills, on an ancient typewriter, are a condition! A few hearts sink, but nobody leaves.

What am I doing here? A telephone call at work, from a casting agency, had asked for a gentleman with a German accent. No problem, obviously, if that was the only qualification expected. Now I'm here, like everybody else, to meet the director; I, a former actor among so many working and struggling ones, as is undoubtedly the lot of most of them.

Mixed emotions for me, to say the least; back home again among the people whose fragile existence I feel I know more intimately than any other and which now promptly has its effect on me — I, too, become ever more nervous and unsure of myself the longer I wait. On a more rational level, of course, there is equanimity — after all, I'm only a guest here, with nothing to lose, but then again, gnawing on such confidence, comes the notion that I'm a traitor who has left the profession for a steady job and who has really no right to be here anymore.

One after another the women are called in; we hear a few clacking rounds on that typewriter and out they come again, smiling through an air of defeat. Then, at last, it is my turn, not with the wretched machine that sits like a sacrificial altar in the middle of the room, but on a chair at the director's desk.

Would I read these few lines, please? — Bland lines, indeed, so I read them blandly. — Yes, thank you, I'm told, but you see: this man, whose part you're auditioning for, is a Jew, and these lines from a letter tell him, implicitly, that his mother and his wife are on their way to Auschwitz; it is written by an Irish official who also asks him for repayment of the postage costs the Irish State has incurred in supplying him with this information. The film is a documentary about Jewish immigration or, indeed, the absence of it into Ireland during the 1930s and '40s — that changes everything. I read those lines again, and the director is happy. And I get the part, all ten seconds of it.

So, this time it's a Jew I play; last time it was a Nazi. For many years now, my inner life and, to a degree, my professional one have been preoccupied by these extremes, the Nazis and the Jews, the Jews and the Nazis. As has been the case for my whole generation, and for many more to come. So I can safely claim that my life was geared towards reading those lines now, in public, in front of a camera. I, too, am happy about that.

As I leave, the waiting-room and the adjoining reception area are crammed with male actors, a phalanx of dark-suited, well-groomed, good-looking men, ambassadorial and public-servant material galore. The men's behaviour towards each other is different from that of the women; sterner, their glances have a more testing, testier glint about them, a haughtiness that is aware of imminent humiliation. I make my way through the hiring fair and, overcome by a totally irrational, totally inappropriate feeling of achievement, I take flight.

The Undertow

After closing time our small group quickly swells to unmanageable proportions, and somebody decides to let us in. We're herded first through a narrow, dark passageway, then across a dank courtyard sparsely lit by blinding spotlights, where bouncers eye us with bland faces, and finally down a flight of stairs into a huge, subterranean hall. The lights are few and futile against the overpowering blackness of the place. On first glance it appears to be boundless. But on opposite sides there is the lure of sparkling bars, and soon all life congregates there. In front of us is a small black stage, flanked by towers of oversized black loudspeakers. Most of the audience have been drinking, and continue to do so. And smoking, in no time the air has turned grey. No, I'm not a regular at such events; in fact, tonight is the first time after many years, and I can see that I'm probably twice the average age. But tonight I just had to be here, and like the rest of the crowd I'm waiting patiently, impatiently.

When I first heard tonight's singer on CD, I was so struck by him that nothing but a classical reference would do for me — here was the Orpheus of the Nineties, another reincarnation of the mythical singer the Greeks imagined to give a name, and a fate, to singing so true, so expressive of the human soul in joy and pain, so irresistibly pure and beautiful that rivers, rocks and the living world all listened in awe to the singer

who even sang his beloved back from the dead — almost.
There are, at any given time, innumerable fine singers present
in the world, and we have to be grateful for them all and sing
their praises, but only rarely do we come across a life that
seems to fulfil itself in song completely, in such singing that
our human existence is elevated to a higher plain, made
grander, more noble, more tragic, more wonderful. The genre
doesn't really matter, and admittedly the experience is largely
subjective. In my life I had it once with a classical singer,
Kathleen Ferrier, and once with a rock singer, mysteriously
enough the present singer's father, who died almost exactly 20
years ago. But that mine is a widely shared opinion is
suggested by the fact that the first album of our singer, called,
most fittingly, *Grace*, has been voted 'Best Album of the
Year' by several of the big music magazines and that he has
already collected, globally, a huge following — witness
tonight's packed house in Dublin.

By now it's almost one o'clock. The warm-up act has done
its laborious bit, unrespected, unrewarded, and has
disappeared. All of a sudden he is there; a young man who
fumbles around on the stage-floor with cables and plugs,
straightens up and steps to the microphone. The audience
explodes into a scream, and the voice begins its flight.

And its fight, with a noticeable cold, to begin with, and
perhaps with exhaustion, as this is the last concert in an
extensive tour. Still, the magic soon comes through, the
spellbinding presence of a man's soul, fully alive. The range,
both tonal and emotional, is staggering, from a deranged howl
to the tenderest of whispers. The real fight, though, is with the
audience, a noisy, desensitised, distracted lot, forever gabbing,
forever toing and froing between the bars and the loos. The

music, at this late hour, is consumed as a commodity, as a background to more urgent concerns — the couple blocking my view, pints and fags in their hands, are all but devouring each other with the rest of their bodies. The band fights back with a volume of sound which to my ears is plain punishment. I put my fingers into my ears — probably the only one to do so in the whole place — but to no avail; my guts are reverberating with the drone. Fortunately there are also some quiet songs, and during one of those a shocking incident occurs; the singer is weaving a sustained note of white-burning silk; there is, for once, total silence when a single word comes flying, like a knife thrown, from the crowd at one of the bars — 'Fake!' Even in these brutish surroundings, the word creates a momentary shock, hushes subdue the would-be assassin, because that's what it was, an attempted stab at the singer's very heart. Yet he sings on, apparently protected by a shield of concentration.

What's he doing here, then, my new Orpheus, in this sulphurous hellhole — if we leave aside for the moment the business contract that obliges him to stand there and do his thing? Why is he wooing this assembly of minds, restless in the throes of quite unmusical demons? The only answer is, as with any true singer: he is singing for his love, which is just another way of saying, he is singing to save his soul. Singing, as we have witnessed often, can be a way of living and dying, both at once, like a flame, and what I see and hear tonight, through the screen of chatter and smoke, is that vulnerability incarnate. After all, Orpheus too came to a horrible end, being torn to pieces by the jealous women of Thrace, his homeland.

The concert ends; once again the singer has sung into the wilderness, bewitched its denizens; there are hungry shouts for more, and more. And then another frightening moment: suddenly the singer takes a few steps back, rushes forward and hurls himself out into the void. For a split second his young, muscular, glistening body hangs in the air — a salmon, leaping upstream against the current — then he falls into a thicket of raised arms, which opens up and closes over him. So that this hunger, too, is stilled.

Two years later Jeff Buckley is dead, drowned accidentally in the Mississippi, pulled down by the undertow from a passing ship. He died singing; the song the Old Man River smothered in his mouth was Led Zeppelin's 'A Whole Lotta Love'. The grief among his followers is, in my case, made heavier by a vague feeling of guilt — for my foreboding.

Galapagos!

One week last February in the headquarters of the Goethe Institut in drizzly, cold Munich, for a training course. Listening to presentations, giving presentations; evaluations, specifications, concepts, projects; short breaks, long talks. And now it's already the last evening — farewell party in the canteen. Salads and snacks. And lashings of good wine. After first mixing and milling, people gradually gel in groups around lamp-lit tables, islands of intimacy in the darkness encroaching from the world behind the glass walls. I join two men at one of the tables; I want to congratulate the older, grey-haired one for the talk he had given on the most frightening aspect of the whole course, for me, anyway, that of keeping proper accounts. He had made the subject almost interesting; his wit and large-mindedness, his humanity had taken the dread out of the matter, and he had done it all in the most beautiful German I had heard spoken for a long time. I knew his name was as German as they come, Drechsler, but there was a foreign air about his pronunciation which made it so attractive.

He blushes at my compliment; he had only learnt the language some 20 years ago, at the very institute where he is now head of the accounts department. My praise opens the floodgates of conversation; soon all three of us are dipping deep into our personal histories. Yes, he is an Ausländer of sorts, his father was an Hungarian Jew who had moved to Prague where he met his wife. They had both survived the concentration camps, she as a forced labourer, cleaning up Hamburg after the fire-storm, his father surviving the horrific death marches of early 1945. They had met again in Prague where my companion himself had then been born. Growing up there under Stalinism, the dashed hopes of the Prague spring of 1968, after which he had fled to West Germany. Shall we have another bottle of the red? Yes, by all means!

The other man has only recently come to Munich, from Poland; his name though is Czech. He had been a member of the tiny German minority who had remained in Poland after the expulsion, suspected and suppressed. If Communism had taught him one thing, he says, it is never to trust anybody! A journalist by training, he has started a public relations agency here in Munich; in the New World of Europe, things are beginning to roll. Cheers!

I'm aglow — places, dates that link up with my own life; I remember seeing the death marches as a child, via Prague we had fled back to Berlin, at the end of our evacuation to what is now part of Poland. Plus my own wife had survived the fire storm. My father, of distant Polish origin, was killed in Hitler's raid of Poland by Polish snipers; my first stepfather, of Czech background, was killed in the battle for Berlin; my second stepfather, he with the Jewish name, had escaped from a Russian POW camp in Poland. And I, growing up in West Berlin, a city steeped in East–West hostility! But now everything has changed, we are sitting here together, while our fathers would have been forced to kill each other! And again we fill our glasses; almost all the other people have left, and we just can't stop asking, listening, sympathising. Oh, the changes, the changes! By and large for the better, we all agree, but there is this coldness in everyday life now, this materialism, this lack of simple human kindness — not among the three of us at this moment, we feel gallons of it running through our veins, it is one of those rare moments ...

Ah, Arne! Come over here, sit down and have a glass of this wonderful red wine! How are you, Arne? It turns out that Arne is very well indeed; he is young, he is of today, and he is sober, too. And with a few lightly spoken words he extricates us from our inebriated wallowing in that horrible Central European brew of history — of Fascism and Communism, racism and nationalism, of barbarism, fatalism, cynicism and murderous sentimentality. Arne has just returned from a three-month contract on the Galapagos Islands, of Darwinian fame, teaching German there to the locals.

German? 'Yes, because of the many tourists from Germany!' And what's it like there? — 'Well, they have many problems with the environment, refuse, water shortages etc.' — Tell us about the wild-life! — 'Well, you can take these guided tours, but they tend to be expensive.' — And what about those famous giant land tortoises? 'Oh, they are everywhere! You see, the upper regions of the islands get quite a bit of rain, enough to keep cattle there. The Galapagos Islands are actually exporting beef! Black and white Friesians they have. And that's where you can see the tortoises, grazing side by side with the Friesians!' — Oh, come on, you're joking! — 'No, that's exactly how it is!' — Imagine!

The Porridge Pot

No sooner had I arrived in Berlin than I was whisked away by my friends; we drove onto the *autobahn* and then eastwards, at speed. Later, on narrow country roads, we were slowed down by falling snow, but finally we made it to where we couldn't go any further east, to Stolpe, a tiny village on the river Oder, Germany's border with Poland. Here, in the low hills overlooking the vast valley, friends of my friends have a little holiday house, and that's where we had been invited to celebrate the New Year.

We found ourselves in an atmosphere of time stilled, speed irrelevant. The landscape we saw before us stretched like that for thousands of miles, up to the Urals and further, a landscape of forests, fields and wide, slow rivers. A huge sky overhead, traversed by changing weathers as the plain beneath has been for thousands of years by tribes and colonisers, traders and conquerors, by armies of warriors and armies of refugees. Yet all we encountered in our few days there was a great stillness, past and present becalmed under an immense blanket of snow.

When we took a walk however, the presence of immanent life became visible everywhere. The area is a national park, and wildlife of great variety is abundant. Written on the pristine white sheet by hooves, claws, paws and tiny feet were the secret stories of the night, the foraging and chasing, the meetings and avoidances, the deaths and the escapes — a story of fascinating complexity, spreading in all directions, without beginning or end. Back in the warmth of the house we mulled over what we had seen, trying to make sense of all the tracks and traces with the help of books. But all the time, within the house and without, my eyes were magnetically drawn to the one object that marks the village from a large distance, the famous *Grütztopp*, the 'Porridge Pot' of Stolpe. Coming from Ireland, one is immediately reminded of the stump of an Irish round-tower, albeit an oversized one, as the thing is some 70 feet high and has a diameter of nearly 60 feet. If you stand in front of it, facing the bulge of red-brick masonry, its mass, its displacement of air have a truly breathtaking, bodily presence. Dating from the twelfth century, it was once the keep of a powerful castle, gone now without a trace; only the tower with its 18-foot-thick walls has withstood the attacks of man and of time. Little is known about its history, but there is a story about how it got its name, in which the fuzziness of history crystallises into legend, telling us perhaps more about what went on here than mere dates and facts could do.

Many centuries ago the castle is said to have been the haunt of a man called Tiloff, a robber baron and generally unpleasant character, who used to spy on merchants on market days and then waylay them on their return through his territory. On one occasion he had observed a trader selling large amounts of veil-linen, a fine, expensive material. When this potential victim passed through the forest of Stolpe, Tiloff attacked him, brandishing his sword. But the trader was ready for him, drawing a pistol he had loaded with a silver button from his wife's dress. The button pierced Tiloff's heart and he fell dead from his horse. His henchmen fled to the castle. When news of their oppressor's death reached the villages, the farmers rose to a man, and soon the castle was taken. Tiloff's men withdrew into the tower from where they threw stones and whatnot down on their besiegers. In the end all they had left was a large pot of freshly cooked porridge. Just then the blacksmith of Stolpe, high up on a ladder, was about to smash down the door of the tower. In their desperation they poured the porridge on him. But with the words: 'We'll soon have that porridge pot scraped out!' he proceeded to kick in the door, and that was the end of the Tiloff reign.

So now we know what the Porridge Pot stands for so steadfastly — for the timeless argument over who is to profit from other people's hard work — robbers or traders. For cruelty and cunning, for individual moments of bravery, for the occasional unforgettable phrase and, of course, for the passing of power from the bloody hands of degenerate gentry into the clean, quick hands of businessmen. With the plain people of Stolpe doing the dirty work. But we mustn't overlook the ingredient of hope in the hotchpotch of history; over there, on yonder hill, where the tower is trailing its long, dark-blue shadow in the white-blue snow, and the setting sun runs its bricky skin through all the hues of red, over there I can see the sparkle of hope as that silver button travels and twirls through the frosty evening air.

On the Rock

The path down the steep slope has to be taken with caution; its surface is uneven and broken, also, at every turn of its zigzag, the view compels us to stop and look around — making us adapt from all the restrictions of our lives to the sudden onrush of space and brightness. We have already left the hill behind us, the houses with their sea-viewing windows, the road with its stream of cars, the DART, carrying people hither and thither; now even our jobs and families slip from our minds as we prepare ourselves for the things awaiting us down there, the only things that will count for us now — a surrender to the omnipotence of the light, a swim in the coldness of the sea. Sometimes that prospect slows us down, but on a warm day it speeds our descent until we take the last few steps almost leaping, arriving at our Land's End, our Cape Finisterre, a place of harsh, bare, glaring simplicity.

Some of us feel the need to quietly celebrate this reunion by our own complete nakedness — if everything else, ambition, worry, status, has fallen away, what is the purpose, then, of dress? But there is no compulsion to do so — clad and unclad, young and old, men mostly, and women rarely, mix in an unrestrained atmosphere and smiling half-absentmindedness.

We move about warily, though, in this environment of rough, abrasive surfaces; we're not at all at home here, despite the liberation we felt at our arrival. Every bit of shelter is welcome. A swimmer looking back sees the honey-coloured granite rocks sprinkled with shades of pink and tan — every niche, every ledge holds one or two of those soft-skinned human creatures, bereft of their protective shells, a whole colony of them, clinging to their rock — a community of sorts, but one of loners, of hermits, of existence drowsily melting into light and silence, the few thoughts in our minds entwining, entangling like Celtic ornaments.

Then an excited call from one of the swimmers: Dolphins! No, not quite, the regulars among us know better; they are porpoises, the little cousins of the dolphins. A small pod of them is resident here in this bay, so close to the capital, at least during the summer months.

We stand in a scattered group, watching in delight the jet-black backs of the animals rising and dipping rhythmically in the glistening waters. Everyone smiles — do we get an inkling of what it might be like to live boundlessly? A line from my favourite poet Paul Celan surfaces in my mind: 'In the liquefied names the porpoises leap' — a poetic image as blinding as the scene we're witnessing: the sea, the very element of life, as a repository of all the perished, starved, slaughtered, departed and forgotten people, an ocean of names, so all-encompassing and present, so real, that real live porpoises are leaping and splashing in them!

Look at us there, in our birthday suits, treading impatiently from one foot to the other, like cliff-nesting birds before their first flight — isn't it easy to imagine that one day each of us, when our moment has come, will walk out there onto the sparkling carpet under the sun, to join the playful porpoises on their journey further and further out into the offing, into the open — never, never to return?

Part IV

Having Arrived

At the Far End

As I look back after so many years, there appears to be a definite westward pull in my life. I grew up in West Berlin, then moved to West Germany where I spent my most fulfilling years, privately and professionally, in two towns at the country's most western edge, one on the shores of the North Sea and the other on its border with Belgium and the Netherlands. When, still at school, my classmates hitchhiked to Norway or the South of France, I went west, without a second thought, as far west as possible. That first journey was followed by several others, and now it's almost 30 years that I have been living here in Ireland. Initially we made a point of getting to know all the different areas of the country, and it was only on our first visit to one particular island off the west coast that the needle of my inner compass stopped dithering, and I felt strangely at rest, even at home. Yet even there, on my many visits, I only feel fully arrived when I have walked out to the island's western end, to revisit the intriguing traces of early habitation there, and to stare out at the empty horizon from where these earliest people must have emerged one day.

When I look out from the cottage where we stay the eye cannot but fix on the other, even smaller, even less populated island which lies just a little bit further west — of course I had to go there, too. When I finally did, a most agreeable feeling of peace descended on me, as if I had come at last to where I had always been, and from where there was nowhere else to go — on this continent, anyway. Or, maybe, in this life.

The far end of this island is a raw and forbidding place. Huge chunks of rock have broken off the grey headlands; looking closely you can make out the faults and cracks where the next big collapses may occur, tomorrow or in a thousand years' time. Breakers explode with a boom in gaping sea-caves. The light and the wind blind the eyes. Towering cliffs magnetically attract and repel the dazed and bedazzled human being. What is it then that lures me to this primeval place, what does my deep self hope to discover here?

One day I take my young son along on a trip out there. He is reluctant to leave his fishing exploits in the harbour area, but then readily warms to our expedition. He runs down the short-cropped slopes of the uplands, his arms stretched out in imitation of the gliding gulls, his blond hair flying in the wind, a ragged halo. Sparkling, white quartzite pieces excite him, as they are excellent for scraping initials into rock-faces. He doesn't tire of doing that, he wants the world to know — he has been here!

The day is bright and warm, but very windy, and when we reach the western cliffs the sea is teeming with white horses; our hands clasped, we can hardly keep ourselves upright against the power the huge space out there is throwing at us.

For our picnic we find a sheltered spot on a narrow promontory where on the windward side, at our back, a tall cliff-face directs the air-stream upwards, creating in its lee a hollow of stillness and eerie silence where we can lie and watch the white, soundless raging of the sea. Cackling fulmars circle and circle in the cove space below us, a timeless clockwork of updrafts and white feathers.

After biscuits and oranges, our hands grope around for something more to occupy them. The usual frequenters of our cosy shelter, the sheep, have left their mark all around us — droppings, as dry and light as dust. I pick up one piece of dung and throw it with a great effort back over my shoulder, as if aiming for the abyss behind us. The wind promptly returns it — in a beautiful, sweeping arch the dirt sails over us, down to the glistening foam below. But what was merely intended as a demonstration of physical laws turns out to be much more for my son — a source of enormous exhilaration. He bursts out laughing as I have never seen him laugh before; he's in the throes of pure, unfettered felicity. Which, of course, delights his father who repeats the exercise, to the same effect. Now we're both throwing dung over our shoulders with all our strength and the wind, obligingly, brings the stuff back — like a swarm of black meteorites it traverses the blue sky on its way down to the foam, accompanied by my son's ever-renewed jubilation. Is it the absurdity of what we are doing that has this effect, the ridiculous contrast between our strenuous effort and the splendid failure into which it translates? Was this the purpose, perhaps, of my long westward journeying, this revelation of mindless mirth, in the face of nothing but the elements? I don't know, but I did not rationalise while we were at it; I threw more dung. And to my dying day I will see it before me, the child's face, luminous with joy, his dark eyes gleaming, madly, blissfully.

Cast-outs for the Night

The curragh races in the little harbour town on the west coast had attracted a large and high-spirited crowd but, as happens so often in that part of the world, the weather in August was a spoilsport; fog, literally, wrapped up the event. After a few yards the boats disappeared into the mist only to reappear, one by one, close to the finishing line when the actual racing was over and done with. The commentator in his makeshift booth on the harbour wall high above our heads tried to compensate for our frustration by imagining pitched battles out there in the mist, but the frenzied loudspeaker voice only accentuated the absurdity of it all. Then the mist turned into a drizzle, the crowd gave up on the event and looked out for other pleasures; there was a pitiable little funfair in a soggy field for the small children and, of course, the pub for the bigger ones.

My 12-year-old son and I, who had come over together with the family with whom we stayed on one of the islands, drifted here and there and finally lost contact with our friends who themselves were drawn in all directions by the many tasks and joys of a day on the mainland. So it happened that at 11 p.m. Aengus and I found ourselves homeless, in a strange town, in the middle of a soft Irish night. All the guest-houses and B&Bs were full. We did not panic, however, as we were by now sufficiently used to the ways of the west to be confident that some solution to our dilemma would offer itself. What about the boat on which we had come over, for instance? We made our way down to the pier and climbed on board — all the available dry space there was taken up by heaps of open-mouthed drunks. Back on the pier, in the driving drizzle lit by a single lamp, it became clear that we had a problem. My eye fell on the race-commentator's booth perched high up on the quay wall. Why not try it? We clambered up to it and — bingo! Half of the floor was wet, but the other half was dry and safe, protected from the strong wind by sturdy canvas. There was a chair, a table, a lot of empty Guinness bottles and litter but, magically, also a broom to clean up our section where we then made ourselves as comfortable as the hard boards would allow — a home at last. One with three walls of canvas; wall number four was non-existent, the drizzly dark.

Underneath our abode was the car-park; after closing time — with extension, of course — the drama of departure: shouting and screaming, doors banging, tires screeching; stranger noises too, people relieving themselves of many a pint and, in the end, from out of the last car, the strangest noises of all, at least for my 12-year-old, sighs and grunts, people making some sort of love. All life was happening down there, and we were in the middle of it, nay, hovering above it, an invisible, secret audience. Then, finally, silence, deep, dark silence.

We were alone, the two of us, father and son, glowing with joy and satisfaction; cast-outs for the night, we had mastered our fate, that's how we felt, and as young and old men do in such situations, we felt like heroes; we talked proud nonsense; we joked and giggled; we peed together down on the world — two lovely, glittering arcs vanishing into the dark — and we took care to synchronise our turning over in our narrow sleeping-quarters. Towards morning it got cool, and as my jacket was the only covering we had, I took my lanky fellow into my arms as I had done so often when he was small, and once again, and for the last time, I felt, he slumbered in the hollow of my body. I did not sleep, savouring instead this moment of outgoing closeness.

A misty dawn brought visitors to us: a robin, later a wren, both eyeing us blackly. Gulls passed, then passed again, peering into the strange stage-box where two human beings were playing bit parts tonight, for empty space, for the birds. Finally I nodded off too. We awoke into a blazingly bright, blue morning, and climbed down from our perch, refreshed and happy to the bone. We soon found our island friends and had great difficulty in absolving them from their withering embarrassment. They really shouldn't have worried — their little forgetfulness had dropped us into the middle of the world, and presented me with the most unforgettable night of my fatherhood.

Halfway up the Hill

On a sun-drenched day last summer I climbed the steep western slope of Knockmore on Clare Island. A steady surge of warm air from the Atlantic was gently nudging me upwards. Halfway up the mountain, in the heart of a hollow, I reached a set of earthworks, small oval enclosures, the remains of booley-huts, where in past centuries young members of the island community used to spend the summer season herding their cattle. I lay down in one of these troughs, resting, as it were, in a bath of earthly silence, only deepened by the sizzle of the grasshoppers and the almond scent that rose from the dry grass.

Lifting my eyes to the top of the slope I saw three black spots there against the blue sky, rising and falling, rising and falling: a family group of kestrels, small, lightly built falcons, were riding the up-current there, mock-chasing each other, weaving garlands of wings into the blue. Presently the largest of the three, the female, left their game to do some serious hunting; hovering in the steady breeze like a little black cross pinned into the fabric of the sky, she then swooped downhill, landed on the ground and almost immediately rose again for more hovering and swooping. Gradually she worked her way down the slope as if on a staircase made of wind. Soon she would see me lying here, take fright and fly away. But no — she was hovering straight above my head now, too close for my binoculars to be of any use. I marvelled at the translucent, chequered pattern of her wings and tail; I looked into the black marbles of her downward peering eyes. And she into mine. Unconcerned, she landed in the grass a few yards away, poked around with her beak, and up she flung herself again, back into her element. And worked her way further down the mountainside.

The other two, when I looked out for them, were still at their play. But all at once there was a new presence among them, a dark and dangerous one, a larger bird who flew rapidly and full of intent in a straight line along the hill's crest. One of the kestrels tried to involve him in the game — one flick of the dark one's wing sent him away screaming. This was a peregrine falcon, you could tell it from his raffish pirate's sideburns. At the northern end of the slope he turned abruptly and, in one long, powerful sweep, came back to the southern edge. There, for a moment, he seemed to stop and hesitate, before I realised, with an electric shock, that he had folded back his wings and was stooping right into my upward gaze. In a split second he had burst through the focal depth of my binoculars; I lowered them, and as I ducked, he was already there, passing only two or three feet above my head, the whirring sound of the air in his feathers like muffled thunder. He swerved, looked back, and disappeared over the rim of the hollow.

What was going on here? A minute ago one of the denizens of this hillside had not deemed me worthy of alarm, and now another had taken or mistaken me for prey! I was experienced enough as a birdwatcher to know that both incidents had been highly unusual. Was this a special moment, the hour of Pan? Had I been allowed back, for a leap minute, into the wild state, a fellow creature, living a life from chance to chance, between being taken and being spared?

I was interrupted in my confused musing by some very strange calls, such as I had never heard before: a deep croak, melting into a canary's sweet trill. Presently their originators came into view — two ravens who had spied me and were warning each other against the intruder with this weird concoction of sounds. To me, in my disorientation, they were like clowns, mocking me, mocking me, mocking me …

The Isle Is Full of Noises

One always gets them slightly wrong, those classical quotations. I felt sure that Shakespeare in *The Tempest* had written: 'The island's full of voices', but, no, Caliban says: 'The isle is full of noises', a subtle, but important difference. Or is it, really? On an island? Voices coming across the water from a boat, or from inside the pub, or from a man on the hill shouting to his dog, can be just noises, soothing, reassuring, but hardly registered noises, as much part of the landscape as grass or stone. True noises, on the other hand, can be loaded with information: the roar of a helicopter would indicate that somebody at the western end is seriously ill, or has met with an accident; a car passing early in the morning means that So-and-So is going out fishing or, if it's in the other direction, that he is more than likely drunk, and there is a whole story to that, too. And the braying, bleating, warbling and cawing that go on all year round — are these voices or noises? Just now the gales outside this cottage are having a fierce argument with the roof and chimney, the outcome of which gives cause for some worry; the hissing sound in the bushes near the window tells me it is a southwesterly wind, and the silent glow of the coals in the open fireplace reminds me of the one voice that is now missing in this ensemble, that of John 'Lizzey' O'Malley who until recently lived in this cottage. He was called John 'Lizzey' after his mother Elizabeth, to distinguish him from all the other Johns and the many O'Malleys on this island.

For us the cottage and the voice were one; entering through the low door meant hearing John's firm voice making us welcome, even before our eyes made him out in the half-light. It's an ordinary West of Ireland cottage, with a bedroom at either end of the kitchen-cum-living-room; what makes it unusual, at least in my experience, is that it is built into the slope of the hill and that, for some reason, a complete levelling of the floor had not been possible, so that its interior still follows the incline of the hill — entering it, you literally walk *up* to the fireplace. The table too has the same gradient, writing this I'm actually pushing my pen against the lean of the land. Things tend to slip, shift and roll in this house; gravity makes sudden grabs for you, you have to watch your step, your balance, just as you have to out there, on the body of this island, among the slippery seaweed on the shore, the treacherous surface of the bog. The house is as much part of the landscape as its former owner was — an uphill house, an uphill life. John was a farmer and fisherman; in his youth he had been, like so many men around here, a labourer in Scotland; in his later years, again like so many of his generation, he had been a keeper of the oral tradition, a storehouse of songs and stories, anecdotes and sayings, a man of many voices, but also one with his own, highly original turn of phrase, sense of humour, and increasingly Beckettian view of life. Even when he was alive, people used to quote him, express themselves 'the way John Lizzey would put it'. Now that he is gone, his house seems to float in limbo — still holding his presence in every detail, but also lost, lonely, without purpose. After some time it will let go, and crumble or, as it is to be hoped, it will be transformed into a holiday home for summer visitors, like myself at this moment.

It is to this special place, with its vivid memories, that I have brought a fascinating find from a neighbour's house: the centenary edition, from 1994, of the *Mayo News*. I want to search in it for information about Clare Island, John Lizzey's island, of which he was so proud. John was born in the year 1900, he was as old as the century, and any item I might find would tell me something about the world he was born into, the times he experienced, indeed it might give me a fuller understanding of John Lizzey, the man, now that it is too late.

Surprisingly, the editorial part of this special edition actually opens with a contribution from Clare Island:

A Clare Island Evicted Tenant's Lament

Clare Island must I leave you now and go across the sea,
Clare Island must I leave you and wander far away,
The little boat that bears me off is sailing from your shore,
Your charming hills and caves and cliffs I never shall see
  more.

When times were good and I in health I always paid
  my rent,
I tilled the land and hooked the fish and never a penny
  spent.
But now the blight destroys the crop, the fish desert
  the bay,
And I must go because the rent I can no longer pay.

Alas, I'm broken down in health, my children, they
  are weak,
My wife, the gentle creature, from hunger scarce
  can speak.
Yet in this sad condition the world we have to face;
Did mortals ever see before so pitiful a case?

For over thirty years I was a rent-creating tool,
For landlords and for agents I was working like a fool.
If to another master I had half so faithful been,
I would not now be cast off like a worn-out machine.

Ah! Justice-loving Englishmen, in every other land
Between the tyrant and oppressed you always take your
  stand,
Your influence is ever used for justice and fair play,
But here alone in Ireland 'tis all the other way.

Ah! Englishmen, if you but let the scales fall from your
  eyes,
The wrongs you do in Ireland will fill you with surprise.
Deceitful, rotten, false you'll find the class you trusted
  best,
While good and true and honest are the people you
  oppressed.

(20th May 1893)

It's not for me to try and figure out where, on the scale of
public opinion in the early 1890s, between Home Rulers and
Fenians, this piece of socio-political poetry should be placed.
The last stanzas in particular seem to me a potent mixture of
constitutional reasoning, meekness, even flattery, and, at the
same time, a perceptibly growing sense of frustration and
rebelliousness — a confusion of mind and heart which may
well have been typical of the public mood in those, and indeed
in other, years of Irish history. There are even traces of
Marxist vocabulary — 'rent-creating tool', 'a worn-out
machine' and 'the class you trusted best' — which make me a
bit sceptical of the genuine Clare Island origin of the piece.
One would also imagine a man having other things on his
mind after an eviction than writing a poem about it. On the
other hand — if you have the poetic gift, and Clare Island

always had its share of versifiers — when else would you feel driven to protest in your own and only voice if not under the impact of such a blow? At the very least, the poem proves that Clare Island in those years had a reputation for eviction, and for poetry.

John Lizzey had a good few ballads and poems in a similar tone, usually about emigration and political events and figures, like 'John Mc Bridle', as he pronounced the name of the local hero, McBride. By the time he was born, evictions were, by a few years, a thing of the past, but he liked to tell the story of Nora Daly which goes back to those dreadful events.

Her family had been evicted and gone to the mainland but Nora, for some reason, had returned to the island and stayed there, homeless, roaming the green roads every day, dropping in here and there and living off the goodness of the people. She may have been a bit gone in the head — as always, John was fascinated by the irrational, inexplicable moments of the story; she always slept out in the open and always wore cotton dresses, and the strange thing was — she never got wet! When she was given a cup of tea, she would pour away the liquid and chew the leaves! She died one snowy winter night, again in the open, yet when she was found, the snow had left a clean circle around her body! A hundred years after her death, the poor woman had, in John's narration, already turned into a myth, half-saint, half-witch, Clare Island's version of the Flying Dutchman or the Wandering Jew, a haunting and strangely enchanting figure. Sometimes, when walking the green roads nowadays, one recognises her gentle, bewildered voice in the babble of the stream, nor would one be surprised to see a flowery cotton dress in the gravel pit where she used to settle down for the night. It's the roads of the island that lead you back into the past.

For years, John Lizzey's stray donkeys would have provided a link with the next instalment on Clare Island that I found in the centenary edition of the *Mayo News*:

A Curious and Tragic Incident

A strange and remarkable event took place on Clare Island on the morning of St Patrick's Day. An aged and venerable ass, that had seen better days and had done good service for more than its owner, was strolling at break of day in search of food, and as he passed by the bailiff's house in which Mr Pateen Hoban of Killeenacoff was staying the poor animal had the misfortune of seeing that respected and respectable officer of the law shaving himself inside the window. The sight was too much for the noble brute who instantly dropped dead. Some people think that death was caused by the sheer terror of the dread official; but those who ought to know were of the opinion that the patriotic instincts of the beast were so shocked at seeing Hoban on the historic soil of Granuaile's territory that he could not survive it. Anyhow, the fact is there whatever the explanation.

March 1893

Now, this time I have no doubts about the authenticity of the story; that donkey died his sudden death on the island, maybe not exactly in the circumstances as described, but there was some connection. And then the community set about crafting the story, refining and sharpening it, until the journalist of the *Mayo News* only had to pick it up and publish it, a subtle but deadly piece of political agitation. Even an ass could not stand the sight of the oppressor and made the ultimate sacrifice, on the national feast day, and on Granuaile's, the Celtic heroine's, own territory! Poor Mr Pateen Hoban, not merely boycotted, but literally 'ass-ass-inated'! His life afterwards must have been purgatory for him; surely there were knowing, insolent smiles wherever he went, heehaws and giggles whenever he turned his back.

The story strikes me as typical of the islanders' art of narration, their sense of the macabre, their mastery of ridicule, and the earthiness in their dealings with the greatest issues. I've never heard the story told, but it speaks to me from the page in John Lizzey's voice, and that of a few other voices on the island. It is of Clare Island's cultural essence.

Mr Hoban did not have to suffer long, the next entry from Clare Island does away with him and everything he stood for. It's from the 27th of April 1895:

> Clare Island has been completely released from the yoke of land-lordism against which its people fought many a brave battle, and it is now in the hands of the Congested Districts Board. Mr Doran, the Inspector of the Board, has taken up his residence on the island, and it is expected that during the next few months the islanders will be employed building walls between the new 'stripes' which will be allotted to them. The late land-bailiff of the island has taken his departure for the US. Altogether the prospects of the islanders have brightened considerably and if they co-operate with the CDB, as we have no doubt they will, Clare Island will most probably become a happy and contented spot.

And cooperate they did: 76 new farms were created by reappointing the land; what we would now call infrastructural development gave employment to the islanders; a fishing industry was created. But the most immediate task at hand was the building of the mighty boundary wall, separating individually held tillage land from commonage used for pasture. To this day it is a most impressive construction, seven miles long, six feet high, two feet thick and, although built in dry stone, in most places still in pristine condition. John Lizzey was immensely proud of it; the board had estimated it would take three years to erect the wall, the Clare Island men did it in 11 months! And all they had were their hands, their hand-barrows, and just two kinds of tools: hammers and crow-bars. They worked 12 hours daily, for a shilling a day, and after labouring on the wall, they would come down to their own land and do the necessary work there.

John himself was an incarnation of this work ethic and physical resilience. When we first met him, he was one in a *meathal* of men, saving the hay and making it into one of those house-shaped haystacks they call 'reeks' on the island. He was then 81 years old. He spent an entire hot August day on top of a reek, building it up, work that is hard on your back and your hip-joints, as I know from my own experience. Later, at 86 years of age, we found him on one of our visits digging the lazy-beds for his own potatoes. He even made light of the infamous labour of 'potato picking' for which generations of Irish people went to Scotland. 'The people of Clare Island considered that to be a holiday,' he said, 'whole families went there and had a good time!' He himself never married, living with his father and sister and remaining on his own after they had died.

Each time we said goodbye to him at the end of our holidays, he would announce that next year we would have to look for him in the graveyard. We just laughed that off, saying he was set to live to be 100! Often he turned the conversation to his favourite subject, his father, who had died more than 40 years ago. Judging from John's stories, plus a photograph we saw of him and from other islanders' accounts, Michael O'Malley must have been a most impressive and remarkable personality; one might even recognise in him the shadow of a Prospero. A simple, illiterate man, he possessed a rare and, for an isolated island community, most precious gift — he was a bone-setter and healer, for beasts and men. Those suffering came from far away for his help, like the woman who had been told by all the medical authorities that she would have to live with her pain, or the bishop who had plenty of religious faith, assumedly, but seemingly little in the power of this island medicine man, yet who went away, a healed man, regardless. John always stressed that his father made nothing of his gift, finding it strange that other people did not possess it as well. It was his own, most natural, most instinctive reaction to the suffering of animals and human beings, and he would not have dreamt of charging for the gift that had been bestowed on him. It was touching to hear and see John in his old age speaking with such boyish pride about his 'Dad'. Talking about him, it appeared to me, gave him solace in his musings about the riddle of our mortality, our 'being born in order to die', as he put it. One day he gave me a simple but powerful image of that mystery as it had presented itself to him. One evening he gave a fresh head of cabbage to a neighbour, Big Austie, a giant of a man whose enormous boots we ourselves had unearthed when rummaging in the remains of his cottage. The next morning word came that Big Austie had died suddenly during the night. John went to his house and saw the giant lying stretched out and pale on his bed, while on his table lay that head of cabbage, untouched, green and radiantly wholesome in the morning light.

John himself slipped out of this life peacefully; at least that's how it appeared to the neighbour who found him one morning in his untussled bed, after one of the stormiest nights the island had experienced for decades. The voice which had harboured so many other voices in the past had itself become a thing of the past, a sweet noise in the memory. I like to think that in the tempest of that night, his father, the healer, had at last come back to him and plied his simple art.

Ramona, Come Closer

The two people who met for a few evening hours last summer in a lonely farmhouse in the West of Ireland had travelled long distances to arrive at this accidental rendezvous. She was an American, he from deep on the European continent, from Poland. He was on holiday, she had added a couple of days to a seminar she had attended in Dublin — she wanted to get in touch with the Real Ireland! She was divorced, he was newly separated; she claimed to be happy, he was obviously not; in fact, he had travelled as far away as possible from the source of his bitterness and incomprehension.

They met in the darkness of the stable where the farmer was milking his two cows. When the man arrived he saw a shadowy female figure standing beside the cow and the crouching farmer who, from underneath the big belly of the black animal, shouted to him: 'Here's the very woman for you! She's a physiotherapist!' This because the man had injured his knee on the cliffs earlier that day and was limping badly. It turned out she was an occupational therapist, of little use to a lame man, but later in the kitchen she dutifully knelt down before him on the stone floor and examined the bruised joint. Nothing but time could bring relief here, but she nevertheless, ever so gently, rubbed some oil onto the injured areas and then, first professionally, but gradually less so, stroked his knee and calf with hands that, under her earnest yet slightly absent-minded gaze, turned ever more caressing. Time for him to roll down his trouser leg and start something less engaging — conversation!

It was she who was soon in full flight, giving vent to her excitement about a series of weird encounters she had had in barely one week in Ireland. For instance, there was this man on a street in Dublin who had begged her for a few pence for a cup of tea. In a hurry to get to the Abbey Theatre to buy a ticket for *Translations* she had passed him by, but met him again after having learned the show was booked out. This time he asked, could he offer her a ticket? Stunned, she inquired the price, expecting some exorbitant demand. Instead he asked for a fiver, for a ticket that cost £6.50! And it was a perfectly valid ticket! We were all at a loss for an explanation and agreed it was a mystery. She seemed prone to run into these, to have a talent or a need for them, and so the farmer reciprocated with a few mysterious stories from his locality, which she, the American, took in deeply and he, the Continental, listened to with a slightly raised eyebrow.

It was getting dark in the kitchen. Outside the rain poured down. The range glowed. When its little door opened, you looked into the fires of hell. The two visitors, coming from early-to-bed cultures, decided it was time to depart. But before they left, the farmer put on a cassette, as a farewell, he said, Bob Dylan's 'Ramona', sung by the Irish singer Sinead Lohan. The electric, emotionally charged voice filled the warm room, the nervous waltzing rhythm entered their bodies. The man started to sway with it, as much as his stiff leg would allow. The next moment the woman was at his side, asking for the dance. And then we saw the most awkward waltz — barely touching each other, their eyes lowered, mouths set in a timid smile, moving in circles around the axis of the injured leg, like two animals tethered to the same stake. 'Just do what you think you should do,' said the song, and the woman leaned her head slightly against his shoulder. 'And one day, maybe, who knows, Baby, I'll be back and be crying to you — ' the song ended, and they quickly separated. 'That was the first dance for more years than I care to remember,' she said in a hoarse voice, and he mumbled something like 'Same with me'.

And then they left on their separate ways for their accommodation for the night. Outside it was so dark, they would have to read the road with their feet.

The White, White Rose

There is almost nothing around here that could compare with the whiteness of this rose. Certainly not the whitewash of the cottage where the bush stands, it only serves to highlight the absolute white of the rose. When I look out at the sea — the foaming breakers, in the sunshine, are quite as white, but they flash and are gone, while the roses hold their gleam all through the day, through dawn and dusk, even in the darkest nights I can still make out their pale shimmer. 'Stella Maris' the variety is called, says my book, the pole star to which we turn when we have lost our bearings, and I can't think of a more suitable name. The blooms are not bunched together but regularly spaced, each one resplendent in its own white sheen, against the rich green foliage. It's not a noble rose, belonging, as it does, to the rough Rugosa group; the branches are encrusted with thorns, picking one you are bound to be wounded.

But pick them you must, if only to admire at close quarters their immaculateness, the elegance of the five green sepals, like fingers holding up between them something luminous, fragile and precious. The petals, silvery veined, slightly crinkled and thus many-faceted in the light, are of course the flower's first glory, an untrammelled, loose assemblage of the lightest tissues, of host-like translucence, the smaller ones, towards the middle, even when fully open still half-hiding a sprinkle of gold-dust, the wreath of male stamens, surrounding the stigma or, as the Germans call it, the 'scar', the female part of the blossom, the focus and purpose of the whole splendid show. From the depth of these parts rises the second glory of this rose, a most beguiling fragrance, delicious but delicate, the flower is bathed in it. Yet you only become fully aware of this when you have a few of them in a vase indoors; in the open air the constant breezes of the island dilute the subtle richness of the aroma.

I put four of them into a water glass on top of the fridge, which dominates the room like an altar, opposite the open fireplace. Each time I pass them by, I receive a gentle waft of perfume, like an earthly blessing, or as if the air suddenly smiled. At night I take the little flower arrangement with me and place it beside my bed — why should they sweeten the night air unappreciated? And again, in my tossing and turning, each time I lie on my right side, there is this scent, like a silent, loving presence.

Is it any wonder then that, as a man and on your own, your mind turns to remembering feminine moments — the girl who always, always smelled of roses, the woman who was bewitched by them? Any wonder that from the depth of your memory or your longing, there arises the aura of love-making — those glowing glances and heart-stopping encounters, promises hoped for and perhaps even promises kept, the ever evasive nature of fulfilment, and all the enhancing and then again stultifying power which, for the man, lies in what Goethe called the Eternal Feminine.

There was very little of that in the life of the man who planted the rose and who dwelled in this cottage until a few years ago. He farmed and fished, yet he never married and lived with his sister, a woman knowledgeable about plants and herbs. After her death, when he lived alone, an old man, he was popular with certain Continental lady tourists who enjoyed his gentlemanly manners, his earthy sarcasms, his lack of cant and wealth of anecdotes and well-turned phrases, and who showered him with their easy charm and their postcards from faraway places. That, as far as we know, was all of the Feminine he had in his life.

Although in no way given to sentimentality, he loved his rose and, by always having a few of them in the house, I only follow his example. He died some years ago peacefully, in the middle of the wildest hurricane in living memory. Now I sleep in the bed he died in, and sometimes at night, for a few seconds, the two of us are one in the scent of his rose — the man who is sleeping for good now and the insomniac, the rooted island man and the man between two worlds, the man who never entered the labyrinth of love and he who did and came out at the other end, bewildered, a wounder, wounded.

Oh, the living breath of the white, white rose!

A Ghostly Image

Here is an image as it might appear in a vision: essential, powerful, in stark colours against a background of foreboding darkness, emerging from it just for a moment, like an omen, reverberating in the throes of history, before fading again, leaving the visionary to ponder the meaning of what he was chosen to see.

Except that it isn't a vision at all, rather one of many pictures that can be inspected calmly, in all their archaic simplicity, on the restored, white-plastered ceiling of the Abbey on Clare Island, a building which never was a real abbey, only an off shoot, a sort of colony, maybe a penal one, of the Cistercian Abbey Knockmoy on the Mayo mainland. While it probably never held more than half a dozen monks at a given time, this humble little community has bequeathed to the island an equally humble but unique treasure. Medieval wall-paintings have rarely survived in Ireland, but among the small handful of examples extant, the Clare Island frescoes are totally beyond compare.

You might expect saints in long robes, angels and scenes from the scriptures in such a setting, as you can still see them in monasteries everywhere else in Europe. Nothing like that here, though; instead, animals, simply but realistically drawn — hounds, horses, birds, stags, hares; a raid, it appears, on farm animals, where cattle, goats and pigs are being driven away by mounted raiders, shooting with bow and arrow. The beasts of the Earth are mixing with those of the mind, of Heaven and Hell: a garish dragon, in spiky, bloated triumph and, right beneath him, another one, vanquished; a pelican, feeding her young in the mythical way, with the blood from her heart. But through the tension of it all, the anguish, the inaudible screams of hunt, and theft, and kill, there is a wafting of sweet notes: musicians, seated on beautifully crafted, three-legged stools, bring balm to the driven soul. The best-preserved image is the harpist, joined now by the rediscovered organist, on his primitive ten-pipe instrument, together with his bellows-worker, both in furious action.

The cycle is a fragment, albeit an extensive one; many pieces are missing though, and some images can only be seen as incisions made into the still-wet plaster, the colours of the original painting lost forever. Future visitors, for instance, will struggle to make out the spectre of an angel, holding up the scales of the Last Judgement, complete with the Jaws of Hell waiting underneath, surely an anchoring image in the concept of the whole. Art historians, no doubt, will have a field day once the restoration, by a team of European experts on commission by the Office of Public Works, is finished, hopefully later this year.

But back to the first mentioned, the 'visionary' image, the one that epitomises, for me, the underlying theme of conflict and strife. Here are two fighters, barely ten inches tall, two wrestlers, to be exact, their upper bodies thrust against each other, arms grabbing for, holding on to the opponent, heads resting on the shoulder of the other — two men, locked, for seven centuries now, in their hostile embrace. One is painted blood red, the other a rich yellow, so it looks as if the yellow man has a red, and the red man a yellow head — the heads of fighting men and women are interchangeable.

So here, resurrected from layers and layers of encrustations, overpainting and organic growth — the cover-up attempted by weather, nature and man — this image has finally returned to us, on this island off Ireland, to haunt us in the light of our own days. Oh, and there is one more little detail: the ravages of the centuries have reduced the physical integrity of the two fighters; they are both down to one leg each. Their struggle is what keeps them upright. It is their crutch. They will never walk again, separately.

Farewell to the Rick

They are now all but gone from the Irish countryside, the great hay-ricks in the haggard, the hay-garden, squatting reassuringly close to the farmhouse, looking like cosy cottages without windows or doors. Or even, depending on the angle of view and the hour, like ancient animals — mammoths, with shaggy hides, or musk-oxen, their massive heads lowered into the wintry gales. Gallarus Oratory, too, came to mind — the same tapered shape things seem to take on when piled up in an orderly and thoughtful way, the compromise between the human need to build up and the Earth's insistence on pulling down. Yes, most of the hay-ricks have long been replaced by corrugated-iron hay-barns, and they, in turn, have more recently given way to silage pits and the black plastic balls of wrapped silage, to the detriment of the poor corn-crake, the fish in the rivers, the smell of the country air, and the visual appearance of the countryside in general. Even on the western islands, where traditional farming methods still hang on, even there it's only a handful of farmers who keep faith with the rick. On our first visit to Clare Island, in the early 1980s, it was the magic shape of the 'reeks', as they are called there — the name and shape, echoing the other 'Reek', the holy mountain of St Patrick which dominates the area around Clew Bay — it was their magic shape, their stern and weathered presence that we tried to capture in drawings and in photographs. That had been around Easter when they were nearing their end, their rounded forms by then dramatically cut and quartered. When we returned in the summer that same year, we arrived just in time to find a *meathal* of men in the process of transferring the hay from the cocks in the field to the haggard where one rick was already finished and a second one steadily growing. I joined them with a spare fork, and so had my first experience of such work. And now I may well have had my last. Here, too, a hay-shed will in future make building a rick unnecessary. And so — if the rick, and with it the very thing itself, hay, is doomed, and there are possibly good economic reasons for it — let their passing be unlamented but not altogether unmourned. Here then is a farewell to the rick.

If hay should prove a thing of the past, well then, the year 1995 was its chance to go out in a blaze of glory. After weeks of wonderful sunshine, dried by wind and warmth, perfectly seasoned, crisp and scented, it awaited its winter storage. The day when the rick is built is one of the key dates of the farming year, one of the decisive, unrepeatable actions of the calendar. All the work of the previous two months: the cutting of the grass, the 'lapping' of the swathes for better, quicker drying, the making of the cocks and their covering with the neat, handkerchief-sized head-scarves — all this was aimed at that single, all-important date, so crucial for the fodder needs of the coming winter. So the day has to be carefully chosen, in bad summers literally snatched from the claws of the weather-beast. Too much wind, for instance, is an obstacle, a shower in the middle of building the rick would be a disaster. Sometimes the decision is made at the drop of a hat. Not for nothing it's called 'saving' the hay.

But, of course, the summer of 1995 caused no such problems, the chosen day was just one in a seemingly endless line of ideally suitable ones. First we had to prepare a base for the rick, a 'track', traditionally a layer of branches which will serve as insulation, allowing the air to circulate underneath. Even after the stack is finished and the hay load has pressed down the track, there is still a springy feeling underfoot when you stand on top of it; it's a lovely, lively, functional message your body, your sense of balance receives from down there.

Onto this track, the contents of the cocks are placed, lap after lap, layer after layer. They, by the way, are not called layers but 'lines'. Gradually the pile grows, lifting me up with it. Soon every forkful becomes an armful of hay for me, I embrace the warm, sweet-smelling stuff with its 'perfume you can't remember or forget', as the poet Brian Lynch says. I try to put each armful in its proper place, but my main job is to slowly walk up and down the track and trample the 'heart' of the rick into a firm core. Only a well-trampled heart, crowned by a well-appointed 'head', will divert the falling rain and make it run off. A soft heart, I'm told, will turn soggy and will mould and rot.

Slowly this thing, this monument made out of the most ephemeral of building materials, out of dried grass, is gaining height and taking shape. A monument to survival itself, a monument to food, made out of food. The upper lines are getting gradually and, it seems to me, naturally, narrower, as a kind of roof-shape appears, the head of the rick. A final, single line forms the roof-ridge. Meantime, the flanks of this hay-creature are several times cleared by hand of all unruly wisps of grass, beaten with the fork and combed with the rake — grooming work on a patient beast.

'To run the rain', a kind of shoulder is sculpted into the sides of the rick, at about half its height, a 'skivvle', as it's called, and a fairly steep one, too. Beneath it, the sides of the structure recede so that the water drops from the skivvle to the ground at a good distance out from the base. The next, and last, job is the thatching of the rick with freshly cut rushes. Here again critical nuances are to be observed: straightforward bundles of smooth, hard, green rushes, as one might imagine, are in fact not suitable, rather they should be mixed with some fresh grass which, in the process of drying, holds the slippery rushes together like so many fine threads. And the rushes come in *two* suitable kinds: there is the common sort, the one that covers ever larger expanses of Ireland, and of Clare Island too, and a rarer, more delicate one, with many pretty, star-shaped flowers. The islanders call it *cronnag*; despite its fragile appearance it has more substance, shrinks less, and is particularly well suited to cover the uppermost line, the crest of the rick's head. Starting from there, from the top, handful after handful of rushes are stuffed into the hay, each overlapping the next one like a slate, until the rick has a brand-new, green and shiny wig. And all it now requires is a hair-net. An old, discarded fishing-net will do the job; weighted with stones, it will secure the precious cargo in the fiercest of winds. Now the work is finished, the mind can relax. There is one worry less about the forthcoming winter.

In good weather, it's beautiful work, if I'm allowed to say so, work for two people, maybe a young couple at the beginning of their life together, working hand in hand and mind in mind, gently intertwining words and work. Family work, indeed, when all its members do their bit, in their common quest for perpetuity.

And where there are people, there's competition too. Hay does not throw up a physical challenge like wet peat or clay, so people put the challenge on themselves and often lug incredibly large loads from the cocks to the rick — deeply impressing the likes of me. Because I, holiday-maker and city-dweller, I'm the clumsiest farmhand imaginable. To begin with, I have no plan of action in my head; all I can do is guess the next step from what I hope I've understood was the last one. Regularly I guess too late, too short-sightedly, or just plain wrongly. Linguistically too I'm handicapped. What I'm told to do is often puzzlingly abbreviated or coded in the local brogue, never mind veiled in the well-known Mayo slur. And there are also words in use which I have never heard before, words only ever used in this specific context. Often enough I misunderstand instructions; occasionally I do the opposite of what I've been asked to do or, in my disorientation, I just do something, anything, that comes to mind, because at the moment I'm simply lost. It is truly humbling, having to realise that the most natural things have become alien to me, for example the likely behaviour, over time, of such a simple material as hay, or the proper use of such basic tools as forks and rakes. It is little consolation to tell myself I'm struggling here as a representative of modern urban man, completely dependent on clear 'communication' in small, clearly outlined steps, with my intuitive understanding gone to the dogs. So wedded to my blatantly insufficient intellect am I, that I'm really only useful as a dead weight, as the trampler of the heart, something I do with dedication but also, in the August heat, with too much effort and toil. As for the fork, with its long prongs, I swing it around in such a way that I become a danger to myself and others. In short, almost everything I do is wrong or, what is equally embarrassing, not quite right.

Nevertheless, in the end the rick stands there, bulky and proud, sound as a bell, which is exactly how it looks, when you think of the hand-bells of the early Irish monks. The reason, of course, is that the other, the farmer, the friend, my country *alter ego* as I sometimes like to think, has done the essential work of loading and shaping, of compensating for my shortcomings. Despite all the instructions that simply bypassed me, he just kept going, with a joke and with unshakeable patience, largely unaware, I would think, of my inner turmoil. For he, you see, is in full command of the procedure, he knows the before and the after; in fact, with him it's not a matter of knowing, of consciousness — rather every muscle, every bone in him is so soaked with experience, he would find it almost impossible to make a mistake. With every movement he uses only as much strength as is really needed; by the end, he shows hardly any strain, while my head hums with the heat and the bother of frustration. Like cog-wheels, all his daily activities link into each other; the building of the rick was a particularly big and important but in no way isolated one, as it was for me. It's wheels within wheels for him, and it is his mind that keeps them all in motion. His intelligence has not, as it has for me, withdrawn into his brain — his whole body, all his senses are still infused with it. And that is why finally the rick stands there in all its simple glory — because my *alter ego*, as in a dream, did everything, but everything, right.

It stands there, carrying in its measurements the length of its makers' steps, the reach of our arms, the weight of our bodies. Looking back once more, on our way to an unequally well-deserved cup of tea, I marvel at our opus; a museum piece, I think, in every sense, a perfectly finished artefact, worthy of admiration, and also, alas, a thing of the past, soon only to be encountered in open-air museums and Irish theme parks. Or maybe, some day, even in the Irish Museum of Modern Art in Kilmainham, together with other lost art forms of the Irish past, peat ricks, for instance, or oat stooks — recaptured for Irish eyes by some conceptual or performance artist. Perhaps, to hammer home the message, he or she will spray it black — to make it clear our neighbour, the rick, made out of words from the very centre of our earthly experience — lap and cock, track and line, heart and head — our neighbour, the hay-rick, is no more.

The Universe and I

'We are children of the universe' — what a beautiful thing to say and, as far as we know, it's even true. But both as a concept or as a fact it is most of the time quite ungraspable; the gulf between our daily grind and the immense indifference out there is just too wide. Only very occasionally does the link between the little self and the universe — the All, as it's called in German — suddenly appear convincingly real and close to our skin. And sometimes such moments even occur in quick succession, in one of those baffling coincidences probably well-known to all of us.

Last summer, between many dismal days, there came one extraordinary night, clear and balmy, the moon almost full. I got up from my bed and stepped out of the low cottage door, to look around and, maybe, to feel something. I saw the island landscape around me mildly lit and dormant. The moonlight was reflected by the calm sea, a breathing, shimmering field of luminosity. And when I happened to glance at my arm, I saw that it too was glistening, each hair on it reflecting a tiny bit of moonlight. I realised I was swathed in it, a moon-man. And then I thought, if each hair could reflect the light from the moon, it should also be able to capture the light from every single star up there, invisibly, of course, but imaginably. Why shouldn't instruments sensitive enough to see a burning candle on the moon — why shouldn't they be capable of detecting what might be just a single photon from a distant galaxy bouncing off a hair on my chest? Standing there, naked in my secret caul of starlight, I felt indeed, for a few moments, at one with the universe, if only by reflection, before I began to shiver and returned to the warmth of my earthly bed.

When I came home from my holidays I found a letter in my mail containing the terms — fee, copyright, etc. — for a job I had completed shortly before my departure for the island, translating and recording a number of poems for a not exactly unsuccessful Irish dance show, to be used on their forthcoming tour of the German-speaking countries. The wording was the usual for that kind of contractual document, but towards the end there were some sentences I hadn't encountered before, and they had a dizzying effect on me: the company's rights applied 'throughout the world, in all media, whether now known or hereafter to be devised' — which leaves a huge space to be filled by human ingenuity, doesn't it? — and, so the wording continued, 'to the extent possible in perpetuity and throughout the universe'!

In perpetuity — that took my breath away! In perpetuity, and throughout the universe! Did this mean immortality for me? I had a vision of my own little voice, whispering Irish poetry in German translation, travelling throughout the universe, imprisoned like that famous Russian dog in a shiny space-capsule, eternally helping to generate commercial interest in the All. Eternally. Forever and ever. Why is it that the Hallelujah! which ought to follow is stuck in my throat? And won't come out?

A Story about Sheep

Oh, oh, oh — there's disaster pending! At least that's how it appears to you and me, city people, who have just arrived on this high road overlooking a vast, almost circular bay, here on the coast of Mayo. Two sheep, a ewe and her lamb, are in the process of crossing the sands, one behind the other, slowly, drowsily — they've probably done it many times before. But this time it could be fatal — they are late. From our vantage point we can see what they apparently are unaware of: the tide is coming in rapidly, and they're in danger of being cut off. Presently they reach a heap of kelp-covered rocks in the middle of the bay and are now faced with what we, the observers, know already; ahead of them there is only water. They stand motionless, stunned, staring, side by side now — maybe some deliberation is going on between them, who knows? What I do know is how painful it feels having to rearrange all one's expectations from one moment to the next. The solution they come up with is obviously daft — obviously, that is, to the two of us, overlooking the drama — like gods, you say, distant, all-seeing, and impotent; they're moving out even further, towards the incoming tide, where some more dark stones seem to beckon. And again it takes them a shockingly long time before they realise their second mistake.

We humans up here are becoming angry and impatient; how can these animals be so stupid? Where is now that mystical synchronisation between their own inner rhythms and those of their natural environment, of which we've read so often? Has it been dimmed by domestication, or even broken? Because what they're attempting next is also useless — they're turning back, back to where they had set out from in the first place, and again in that agonisingly slow pace, the ewe, with motherly care, stopping every few steps for the lamb to close up with her. No sign of nerves down there, while we, on our Olympian heights, are getting ever more panicky. We can see that they're already cut off on that side, that their only hope lies in a dash straight towards the shore, in our direction. And even that escape route is rapidly dwindling — from left and right two eager tongues of water are licking towards each other; once they've joined, the sheep will be marooned on a fast-shrinking islet of sand. Now they've reached the point where they have to accept that to return is impossible. And doesn't it drive you mad, how lethargically they respond to that realisation!

But, hold on now — who are we to feel superior to these dumb animals, you and I, for whom it took years to see that we had lost our way! We, who belong to a species that hates nothing more than having to change its material ways! Beings who may well be heading, sheeplike, towards extinction in a tide of their very own making, eyes wide shut, as the man says.

Down there, the mother and child crisis is about to reach its climax. There is no way forward and no way back, and at last the ewe decides on the one solution we felt like shouting down to them all the time, if the gulf between us was not so vast; she turns in, straight towards terra firma, but again so measuredly that those two tongues of water finally join before the animals can slip out between them. Now they're encircled. Another decision, the last one, the one for survival, is called for. After more hesitation, the ewe wades into the water, step by delicate step, always making sure the lamb is with her, even changing course in midstream — the expanse they have to cross seems to grow with their crossing — but finally they've made it, and only the splashing acceleration, the relieved trot they break into, tell of the anguish they, too, must have suffered.

And you and I, high up here on our observation post, we feel like applauding and indeed do so, with a few hand-claps and one or two words of praise spoken into the air. We've just witnessed something instinctual still functioning, after all. The sheep have been spared this time. And so have we.

From a Distance

When they struck the dual carriageway through South County Dublin, they replaced the old, winding road with a much straighter line, cutting off bends here and there, giving them something of the air of ox-bows, calmed backwaters, at a slight remove from the roar of the main traffic flow. At the side of one of these stretches of old road stands a bench, a sturdy, metal one, very functional, not fancy, neither the last of the past nor the first of more to come. It is unique, a bench for itself. Quite literally so — hardly anybody ever seems to be sitting on it — but then hardly anybody ever walks here anymore. In spring, overhanging cherry blossom softens its stern appearance. It's on this bench that I take a short rest when, every so often, I decide to walk into town, it's approximately the halfway mark.

I sit and stretch my legs, feel the prickling sensation of muscles relaxing, of blood rushing to feed in new energy; the mind, too, relaxes; I sit there, feel the west wind arrive on my face, and, if the sun shines, I half-close my eyes and half-watch the cars whizzing past, in packs, from left to right, right to left. Seen through the blur of your eyelashes, from a distance, they all look the same, their speed identical, and some innocent notions rise to the surface of the half-alert mind: why do they all hurry to the left when the next moment they all come rushing back to the right? Isn't there a great superfluity of movement? And look at all those soft-bodied hermit crabs inside their protective shells of steel — are they driving, or are they driven? Is it cars passing, or people? These men and women, isolated from the world in their mobile cages, are they not surrendering part of their human soul — if there is such a thing — to an all-encompassing dream of swift efficiency, itself a mental bubble we all exist in and which we can't escape, least of all out there in the fast lane, encased in one of those bulging bubble-cars. Let's see now — which part of the soul might it be that would be lost? And now the mind is dozing off into realms of utter vagueness — but just then a far from bubbly, rather a big, heavy, huffing shape enters my field of vision, from the right, from the city — a bus, a bus full of people, all tightly packed — or packaged? — all looking earnestly ahead, their minds anywhere but where their bodies are at the moment.

And look, the fellow up there on the upper deck, second window from the front, with the funny hat and the glum expression — probably because of the Walkmans beside and behind him spitting hissing rhythms into his ears — don't I recognise his face? But of course, that's me, that's myself, on my daily way back home to my leafy suburban bungalow! Up there I sit, looking down at myself sitting on a bench, looking up at me, sitting on a bus. The Me in the bus doesn't immediately recognise the Me on that bench down there, so relaxed and seemingly happy, so unbothered, thinking for a moment that I'm a tramp, a homeless person whose abode is that very bench. Well, I'm not, not yet, anyway. I'm only sitting here for a few minutes but, who is to say, if I don't get out at the correct bus-stop, if I get lost on my way home, if I take one or two more wrong turns in my life, I may well end up vagrant and make this bench my occasional address. But do I think such thoughts as I look down at myself, looking up at myself, and thinking them? Oh no, my thoughts up there go straight towards home now, to the welcome I can expect there, or not, and thus I don't see the wave of a hand I give here, down on the bench, the wave of one who is momentarily unattached, homeless and free to wave to anybody, even to myself, passing by.